MEMOIRS ON THE ROAD

MEMOIRS ON THE ROAD

Sue Aspinall

ISBN: 979-83-29010-03-9
© 2024 Sue Aspinall

All rights reserved.
No part of this book may be reproduced or transmitted in any form whatsoever without the prior permission of the publishers.

Cover designed by Sue Aspinall
Maps: © Daniel Dalet/d-maps.com 2024

For Pat

CONTENTS

Map of Entire Route from Morocco to South Africa	ix
Preface	xi
Prologue – Spain *Travelling South and Forwards*	1
1 – Morocco *Beneath the Lion's Gaze*	3
2 – Mauritania *Breaking the Mould*	7
3 – Northern Senegal *Peppering in Some Café Touba*	11
4 – Gambia *One Brick at a Time*	17
5 – Southern Senegal *The Impromptu Festival*	21
6 – Guinea-Bissau *In Search of Chimpanzees*	25
7 – Guinea *Fast Fading Memories of Yesteryears*	31
8 – Sierra Leone *Hunting for the Elusive Elephants*	37
9 – Liberia *Rising from the Waves of Time*	43
10 – Côte d'Ivoire *Watching Basking Sacred Crocodiles*	49
11 – Ghana *The Dreamer's Cocoon*	53
12 – Togo *The Towers of Tamberma Valley*	57

13 – Benin *Travel Protection from a Voodoo Priest*	61
14 – Nigeria *From a Piece of White Cloth*	65
15 – Cameroon *Honouring the Dead in Bamiléké Land*	69
16 – Gabon *Hopes for Lambaréné's Future*	75
17 – Gabon *The Unsung Hero*	79
18 – The Republic of the Congo *Do You Cry?*	85
19 – Angola *The Power of Nature*	89
20 – Namibia *On Diamonds We Build*	93
21 – South Africa *Memories in a Cookbook*	97
Epilogue	101
Thank You Everyone	105
About the Author	107

MAP OF ENTIRE ROUTE FROM MOROCCO TO SOUTH AFRICA

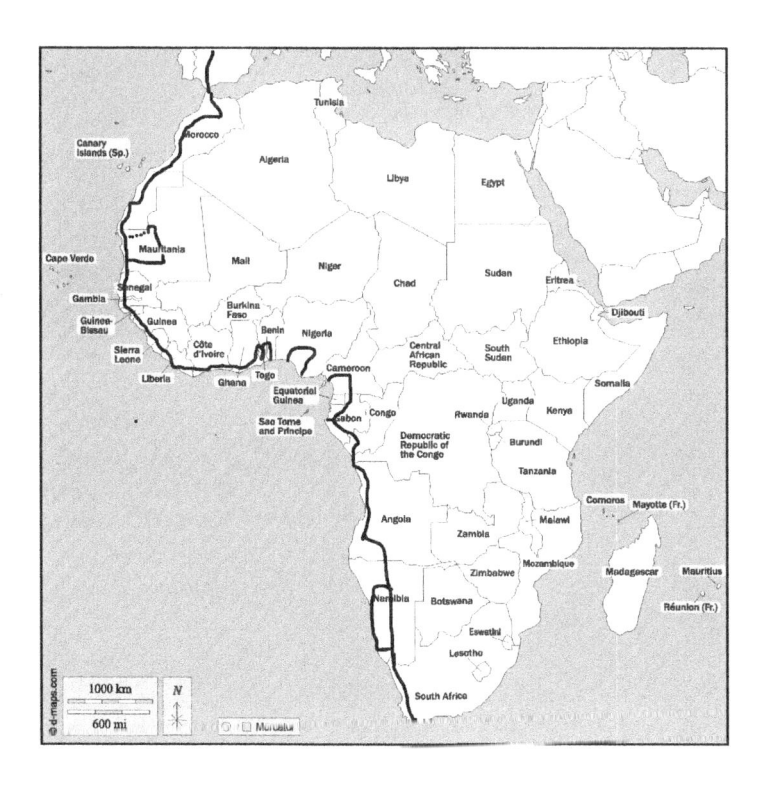

PREFACE

These memoirs were written after the journey from Tangiers in Morocco to Cape Town in South Africa had been completed. What started as just an idea unfolded into a ten-month adventure. From each of the countries visited, I chose to take one memorable experience and build a narrative around it. The chapters are linked by a common thread – my route – drawn on maps at the beginning of each chapter.

The memoirs tell of the people and places that stimulated the deepest of thoughts and that raised questions, provided answers, evoked deep emotions, and created immense joy. In writing them, I hope to share a flavour of the life lived in western Africa from the perspective of its people and of a solo woman traveller.

Sue Aspinall,
The Netherlands,
June 2024

PROLOGUE – SPAIN

TRAVELLING SOUTH AND FORWARDS

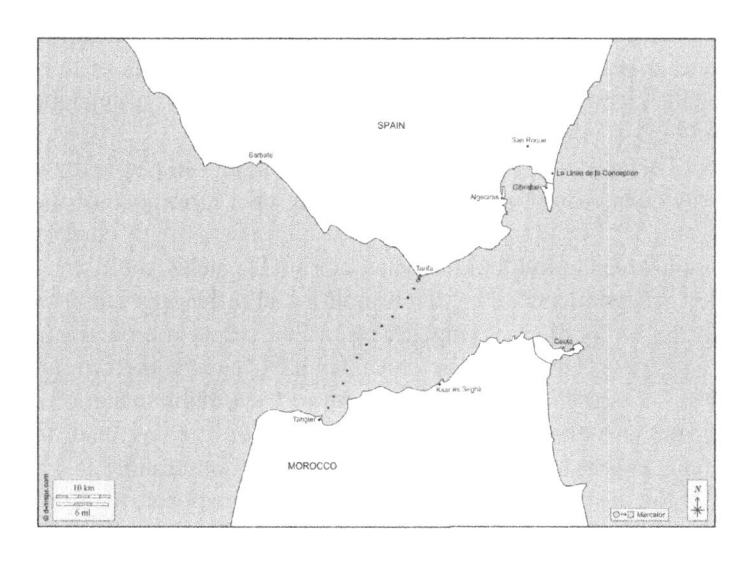

As the ferry pulled out of the Port of Tarifa, I went on deck to watch the coast of Spain drift into the distance and the open sea take over. The sense of excitement was engulfing. This was it; I was on my way and heading south and forwards. I had naively imagined that stepping onto the African continent would immediately bring an onslaught of strangeness, unworldliness, and sensory overload. It was only when I sat on a terrace outside a café in the old souk, amongst local men drinking coffee and smoking rolled cigarettes, that I felt the tingle of newness. Immersed in the world of Tangiers' inhabitants and surrounded by a language I could not comprehend, I leaned into the future I had chosen.

The urge to get on the road had crept up on me over time. I had a deep yearning to break free from what I saw as a stifling post-Covid institutionalised existence in Europe. The peripheral of my comfort zone had closed in on me, and I had begun to feel numb and stuck. I longed for an untethered freedom from routine, expectations, imposed limitations, and the comfort of predictability. I sought uncertainty, unplanned adventure, open-hearted people, new learning opportunities, and challenge. For me, the solution was to wade out of normality, leave it all behind and walk towards a place of intrigue and expansion.

The idea to travel overland from Tangiers to Cape Town was born from a need to address my own ignorance of the countries I would pass through. I was embarrassingly clueless about their individual histories, colonial legacies, their strive for independence, the current politics, and the opportunities available for their young people. What urged me on was a desire to get close to the truth; to experience something of each country for myself by talking to the inhabitants and to hear their stories first hand. I was open to learning, had no expectations and was ready for opportunities to unfold.

The desire to travel overland on local transport came from earlier experiences in countries across the globe. During those journeys I had welcomed the many chances to observe life around me and interact with those passengers with whom I shared seats. These encounters and connections had bound me to the countries I travelled through and provided memorable snapshots of daily life. Travelling on my own had always allowed these meetings to be easy and spontaneous. I had learnt to intentionally reach out, be open, make eye contact, and learn some of the languages. In return, I discovered the rewards of trusting in my own abilities and resources, in the kindness and intentions of the people I met, and in the unfolding process of the journey I travelled. I knew that the destination only provided a desired goal, the purpose and anchor for the trip. It was the richness of the unfolding journey that would settle my cravings and expand my horizons.

1 – MOROCCO

BENEATH THE LION'S GAZE

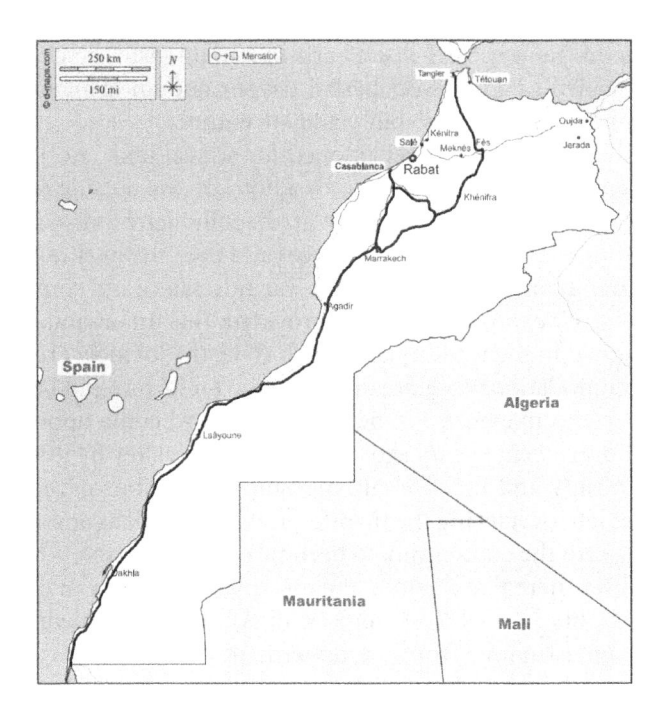

In the film *The Lion King*, Mufasa stood on Pride Rock surveying the valley below and contemplating his responsibilities of kingship and the circle of life – not unlike the legendary lion of the Ameln Valley, whose face was tickled by climbers relishing the challenge of this graded crag. Sitting in the mid-range of the Anti-Atlas Mountains, the stone lion shape was said to be the protector of the valley's people and their water sources. Over the years, it had seen the dramatic changes of the lands below, not least its expansion to new agricultural endeavours and tourist enterprises.

The bus from the Moroccan coast pulled up outside the dimly lit transport office in Tafraoute late in the evening. The bus had wound its way through the lower mountain ranges to drop off passengers at isolated homesteads and hidden villages on the way. As I disembarked, I could taste the change in the air; it had a sweet herbal flavour and an exhilarating freshness, inviting possibility and adventure.

The helpful bus driver phoned for a local taxi, and I was driven into the darkness towards a hotel on the outside of the town. I peered apprehensively at the silhouettes of passing buildings, the fields of stunted trees and then the hazy outline of a mountain range. I hoped for warmth, safety and comfort.

The Chez Amaliya hotel provided this in abundance. Designed in the traditional Kasbah style, the lovingly created accommodation was a dream come true for its intrepid Dutch owner and manager, Lizebeth. Lizebeth had come upon the land over twenty years ago, attracted to the valley by its rugged beauty and the safe guardianship of the lion's gaze. She never left, overseeing the manifestation of her plans and marrying into the community to become one of the tribe.

It was here that I gained the information on how to climb the mighty Jebel el Kest ridge (with Afa-n-Tmezgadiwine as the highest point) from the uppermost village in the valley, Tagoudiche. The trek started with a taxi ride from the bottom of the valley along a switchback dusty road, gaining altitude at each hairpin bend. The driver, Bachir, heaved his old Peugeot round the tight corners and cranked through the gears as we crawled up the inclines overhanging the mountainside. He left me in the village square to catch my breath and marvel at the view of the valley below, strewn with palm, argan and almond trees.

The path to the summit of the mountain began between the peach-coloured walls of the tightly nestled buildings. An elderly woman waved her arms indicating its onward direction and wished me luck. I wondered what lay ahead and whether I could find my way without a guide. Onward seemed to lie through steep gullies and across an overhanging escarpment. Mustering courage, I set off along the path that led over boulders, skirting around cacti and clusters of euphorbia. It then veered across dry layers of quartzite rock, which shimmered in the midday sun. Soon my anxieties disappeared as I followed the faded painted arrows and cairns upwards. The physical exertion was invigorating and the views around me were stunning. After passing a damp cavernous overhang in the rock, I took the route up through a gully where short, gaunt trees spread their knobbly roots between the rocks. This led to a protected plateau from where I began the scramble up onto the summit's rocky ridge.

At the top I stood still and savoured the sheer joy of reaching this vantage point at 2,359 metres. Being able to see across to the valleys on either side of the mountain range was spectacular. The sky was cloudless and there was a slight breeze of warm air. I could not have chosen a more perfect day.

I clambered over to the ancient rock dwellings that had in the past been inhabited by a hermit. To my surprise, the dwellings were occupied as a rest stop by four hikers from the village of Anergui, who had climbed up the eastern route. They invited me to join them, and we huddled together around the small fire on which a pot of tea was brewing. As we drank, they told me about their village and their route to the summit.

Before I began my hike down from the summit, my new companions showed me the best place to view the lion's head. We stood on a flat layer of rock gazing towards its shadowless face from the west. They assured me that at this time on a sunny afternoon one could see the lion's mouth rise into a smile. On this day, however, the face did not flinch. I eventually bid a fond farewell to the hikers and promised that I would heed their cautionary advice for my descent.

Following the same pathway down, I arrived safely at the village and was soon travelling back down the road to the valley below in Bachir's taxi. Later that evening Lizebeth joined me on the terrace at the hotel to watch the sun slowly slip behind the mountain. We watched the gradual change of light fade across the lion's face. As it had for centuries its gaze remained unchanged, serene, regal and protective.

2 – MAURITANIA

BREAKING THE MOULD

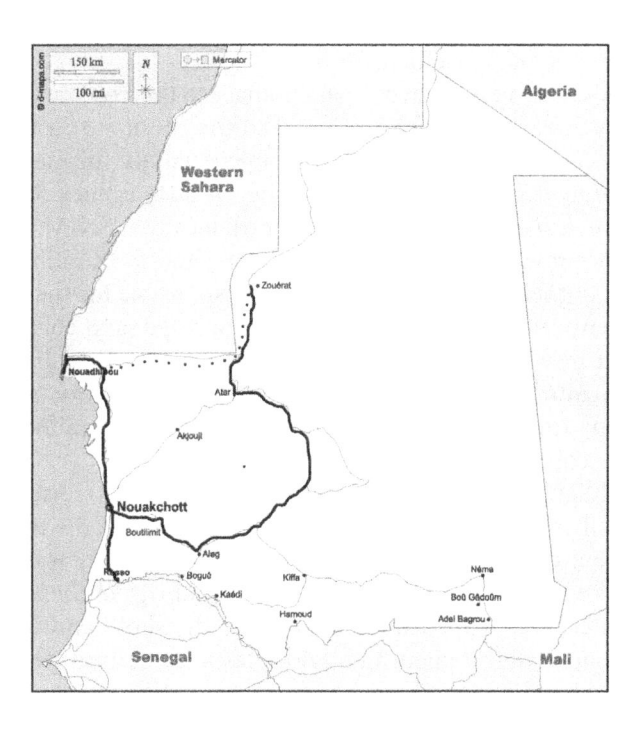

The gentle grinding friction of sandy grains against skin accompanied my every movement in eastern Mauritania. The dry warm air was heavy with the sand particles; they stuck to the inside walls of my nostrils, the corners of my eye sockets, under my fingernails, and inhabited my pockets, socks and eyebrows. I found myself managing the perpetual irritation of itchiness. I craved the anticipated relief of a shower from the relentless grittiness.

Nevertheless, this was the daily reality for my hosts and their fellow citizens in the town of Zouérat. Their lives had evolved to embrace the geographical and climatic conditions of this remote location. Layers of clothing were wrapped tightly around every body part, four-wheel drive vehicles were used to navigate the sand-strewn tracks, and daily sweeping routines kept the elements at bay.

Zouérat's very existence paid homage to the iron ore mines of north-east Mauritania. Central to the country's economy for decades, the mines provided employment for the majority of the town's inhabitants. Owned by the state agency *Société nationale industrielle et minière*, known locally as SNIM, these mines provided work, a salary, a home and food rations to most of their employees. SNIM was responsible for the rows of identical housing blocks painted in a beige sand colour to blend in with the deeper earth-covered tracks that divided them into neighbourhoods. The lime green tin roofs and peeling front doors failed to add character to the uniformity of the configurations.

My guide, Mohammed, led me to number 370, discernible only by a loud rattling sound emanating from the dilapidated aircon unit protruding from the single-storey wall. He knocked and a woman's voice from within gave the signal to enter. We stepped down across the threshold and into a darkened cubicle piled high with plastic containers, textiles and a hand-operated sewing machine resting precariously on a pile of papers. He showed me into a space at the back where a piece of carpet and several mattresses were laid out on the sandy floor to create a communal gathering area for his family.

His sister, Hajar, emerged from the kitchen area and enveloped me in a warm musky embrace. She greeted me in Arabic and immediately proceeded to involve Mohammed in updates from their family based in Atar. My host settled himself cross-legged on one of the mattresses in front of a tray of assorted tins, pots and plastic bottles. And so began the first of many tea ceremonies, where imported Chinese green tea leaves were added to a ration of water boiled on a spluttering gas burner and mixed with pyramid high heaps of sugar. Ceremonially, he began to pour from a height splashes of the sweet foaming liquid into each of the drinking glasses, circling around until all the glasses were half full. He tasted the prepared offering and with a satisfied smile handed me one. I sipped it gingerly under his watchful eye, trying not to gulp it down to quench my thirst.

Mohammed's other sister, Zavia, arrived home from work late afternoon. She nestled into a corner of the room and balanced a bowl of cold couscous on her lap. She scooped handfuls into her mouth whilst updating her siblings about events at the mine. She eyed me suspiciously. Her phone beeped continuously, and I wondered where her attention lay.

I shared this living space with these three wonderful people for two days. We ate couscous together from a large steel bowl set on the floor and drank copious glasses of tea. Slowly they started to share their lives and dreams with me as we used a combination of languages to communicate. Mohammed had studied English and was using his language skills and enterprising spirit to grow a personalised homestay experience for intrepid travellers. Hajar had recently been abandoned by her husband and had joined her siblings as the housekeeper. Her children were with their grandparents in Atar, 250 kilometres away. Whilst keeping house, she took on sewing assignments from neighbours and had hopes to open a workshop in her cubicle by the door. Zavia was less forthcoming, absorbed in her phone and the French lessons she was following. Slowly, she peppered our conversations with granules of information. She had studied electrical engineering in the capital, Nouakchott, on a grant provided by a local sponsor given to the highest achieving student from Atar's high school. Zavia had been appointed by SNIM as one of a minority of women to lead one of their engineering teams. She was the first of this family's women to go to university, to have a salaried position in a company, and be the sole breadwinner. I let her know that I saw her as a role model for others, a courageous woman breaking the mould that others would benefit from. She shrugged her shoulders in response and returned to her French studies, asking if I knew any online forums where she could practise her speaking.

On my final morning, I packed up ready to join the train wagons full of iron ore journeying towards the coastal town of Nouradhibou for export. Mohammed would come with me to the isolated station and help me get on board the train. Zavia went silently off to work.

Hafar sent her greetings to my family. "Please think of me sometimes and visit us soon – we will have a small guesthouse, an auberge, and you will see my sewing shop. Alhamduli llah. All praise is due to Allah."

3 – NORTHERN SENEGAL

PEPPERING IN SOME CAFÉ TOUBA

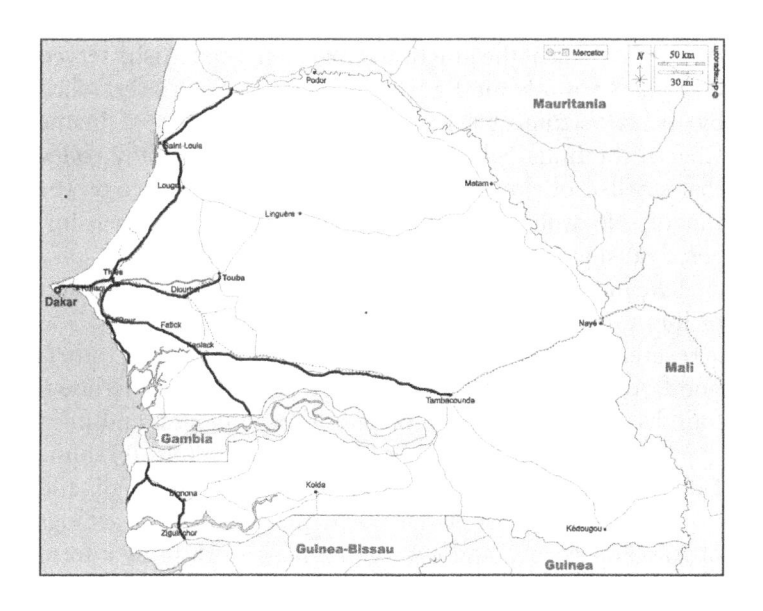

Café Touba is a delicious coffee drink flavoured with pepper and spices. Such freshly brewed cups of coffee were freely available in the marketplace and at the bus station in Diourbel, a town in northern Senegal. Young men could be found there, standing expectantly behind brightly painted trolleys ladened with flasks of steaming water and simmering sweetened milk. Rusty tins concealed a dark assortment of spices already mixed into freshly ground coffee. Piles of upturned espresso-sized paper cups awaited each order. The men skilfully wheeled their aromatic wares around the bustling areas, avoiding the potholes and seeking out the waiting passengers. Aisha told me this was a lucrative trade especially on Saturdays and if one had a regular pool of customers. "My place is different though," she informed me, clearly proud of her enterprise. I was curious to find out more.

Aisha's café Touba was located inside a small, converted storeroom. Its bright green double metal doors opened into the sandy street at the junction of the main road. Aisha served customers from behind a wooden serving hatch overlooked by the two iconic black and white photographs of Mame Cheikh Ibrahima Fall. She served a sweet and frothy coffee that smelled of cloves and left a slight tingle of spice on the tongue. No wonder people queued patiently and then lingered outside on the narrow benches to sip happily.

Like many of the people of Diourbel, Aisha was a follower of Ibrahima Fall, known in the area as Lamp Fall, who was a revered disciple of the founder of the Mouride brotherhood, Amadou Bamba Mbacke. This large Sufi brotherhood, founded in 1883, is said to be one of the youngest and most dynamic, with a structure headed by the Caliph. Ibrahima Fall became the namesake of the sub-order Baye Fall, and as a devoted member Aisha was dedicated to the teachings of Amadou Bamba and considered hard work to be a form of devotion. Following Bamba's advice that devotees should drink café Touba before praying, she had poured her love and devotion into perfecting this coffee art. Her coffee had the identifiable taste of selim, a peppery flavouring that she imported from Gabon. Aisha's business was booming and so was the population of the brotherhood.

The presence of both Amadou Bamba and Lamp Fall were felt throughout the town. Multiple copies of faded photographs of these two revered marabouts adorned homes, workspaces and shop fronts. Jarring assortments of stickers, paintings and photographs mounted in garishly tinted plastic holders dangled from strings of rotary beads, obscuring sections of the front windscreens of every taxi and bus. This unapologetic adoration aimed to yield a better life and provide solutions to problems for its devotees.

The obvious lack of alcohol, cigarettes, music bars and night clubs provided clear clues that a sizable percentage of the population in Diourbel were of the Mouride faith. There was an air of peaceful industriousness punctuated with the calls to prayer that brought a cohesion to this community's daily rhythm.

Fifty kilometres northeast of Diourbel lay Touba, the spiritual centre of Mouridism and the site of one of the largest mosques in Africa. It was the place where throngs of devotees congregated for the annual religious pilgrimage, the Grand Magal of Touba. I was curious to visit this sacred centre and to try to understand a little more about the magnetic force that seemed to be attracting so many of Senegal's population to this religious movement.

Dressed in a borrowed canary-yellow long dress and brightly coloured head wrap, I set off on the bus to join the followers. This conspicuous attire drew curious looks and approving comments. Clearly, respecting the dress code was more important than pampering to my self-consciousness. Reaching to the skies, this revered mosque lay in the centre of a hub of radiating roads. Its central minaret stretched upwards above a large ornate complex adorned with shorter minarets and domes. As I drew nearer, I began to marvel at the 80 years' worth of work, devotion and finance that had been poured into its construction before it eventually opened in 1963.

Hordes of young people had congregated outside the mosque's perimeter fence, lounging on the pavement. They draped themselves over their bulging rucksacks, hugged sleeping bags and shared snacks wrapped in paper. There was a low hum of voices and a patient expectancy in the dawn air, somewhat reminiscent of school students waiting for their residential trip transport.

I stepped around their bodies and belongings and weaved my way towards the gates of the mosque and into its outer courtyard. Unchecked, I strolled alone through the outer corridors and spacious prayer halls, relishing the solitude and precious opportunity. Attendees were rolling out prayer rugs decorated with ruby-coloured paisley Turkish designs, whilst fleets of cleaners armed with sweeping brushes floated silently across the marble floors in their uniform green dresses and scarves. Intrepid starlings flew between the Romanesque Italian columns and under the decorative roofs crafted by Moroccan artisans. The golden dome began to glow, absorbing the sun's rays as they emerged through the hazy clouds.

I watched the devotees and visitors as they started to arrive, climbing the steps towards the prayer halls and gazing wondrously upwards whilst being ushered forwards by their companions. The surge of colour, reverence and anticipation began to flow towards the inner core at the heart of the mosque. The sound of singing merged with subdued voices; a low harmonious chanting of poems and prayers building in volume to an electrifying climax with harmonised repetitions echoing through the corridors. The atmosphere was sublime.

Cheikh Amadou Bamba Mbacke's mausoleum was adjacent to the mosque and the final stop for the devotees making the Grand Magal of Touba. Families and groups clustered inside the cool building, touching its pink marbled walls and deeply carved wooden doors as they passed through. They huddled beside the railings protecting the sacred coffin, some moving forwards to push their faces against the cool metal poles. Crouched and with their heads covered, these followers lavished prayers and requests with outstretched arms towards the marble mound before them. They were joined by groups of religious leaders dressed in white who began to sing relentless poetic pleadings that intensified with momentum and quavering discord.

Feeling as if I had intruded on a trance-like ritual, I moved away to the quietness of the outer courtyard where lines of women and children were enjoying bowls of rice soaked in soup. They ate silently, squatting against the flapping side of the kitchen tent and observing the movement of people through watchful eyes.

As the mosque began to pulse with the streams of humanity gathering within its walls, I slipped out to the pavements beyond. The masses from the morning had disappeared, taken in open-topped trucks to rice fields on the outskirts of the city. I was told that they would stay on the farms for a few days to demonstrate their devotion to Amadou Bamba by working on the land.

I returned to Diourbel in awe of the collective devotion of this religious order and the sustained influence of its disciples. Over time, a sizable percentage of the younger population were attracted to this religious order and its strict teachings of peace seeking, drug free and hardworking devotion. I couldn't help but see its benefits, though deeper questions about its social and economic organisation were left unanswered. Around the outside of the mosque, I had seen several devotees asking for donations. What were these offering used for and how did this practice fit with the teachings of the religion?

The bus station was deserted when my shared taxi pulled into its dusty parking area at sunset. The vendors had left their wooden stalls piled high with merchandise, now tightly covered with fading cloths and secured with knotted ropes, awaiting another day. The coffee sellers were long gone, their trolleys pushed into safe corners depleted of all signs and smells of their treasured offerings.

A portrait of Light Fall gazed down at me from above the closed doors of Aisha's café as I walked past. I wanted to ask Aisha whether she had to tithe part of her income to the religious leaders and if so, the amount. I was curious to know whether individual enterprise was encouraged for the betterment of the owner and their family's life, or whether the religion's social structure encouraged collective giving to improve life for the community as a whole. As a hangover from the colonial times, I was also eager to understand how and why café Touba was so integral to a spiritual movement.

This day had provoked numerous questions and yet so many would probably remain unanswered. A visitor such as

I would need to be content with relishing the delicious fusion of a traditional medicinal spice, a Francophone legacy, and a recipe created by a religious movement in Senegal.

4 – GAMBIA

ONE BRICK AT A TIME

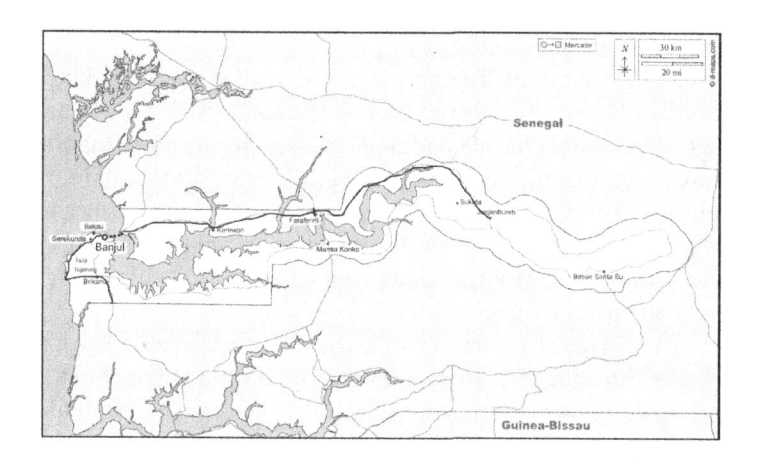

The compound was encircled by a tall brick wall disguised under overhanging creepers and cascades of vibrant bougainvillea. This boundary proudly demarcated the acreage of the property and the social and economic status of its owner. I was greeted at the gate by a snapping dog and Saikhu's warm smile. The incongruency within the compound immediately hit me. Saikhu and his family occupied the simple rooms by the gate, whilst I was shown to a multi-roomed spacious bungalow exuding the faded charm of colonial comforts. It overlooked a mature garden of laden fruit trees and exotic flowers, clearly tended by Saikhu as part of his duties. A shaded seating area next to a small unused swimming pool provided space for leisurely repose. I was introduced to Fatima, Saikhu's wife, as she squatted on the ground over an open fire in front of their home. Smoke circled around two balancing pots, one bubbled with rice and the other emanated a pungent smell of spicy fish. This formed a lavish lunch, later brought by Fatima to the main house, where I was staying, in a huge bowl covered with a bright gingham cloth. Although I felt distinctly uncomfortable with this sudden division of roles and status, Fatima assured me that this was their way of welcoming a guest. We would discuss the arrangement of future meals later in the day.

I had come to Tujereng on the invitation of Saikhu's brother, Baku. The two had bought the compound a few years ago and Saikhu's family had made it their home, investing the money sent from Baku, now based in Europe, to maintain its upkeep. For me, it provided a unique opportunity to stay in a smaller village to the south of Gambia's capital and resort area, and to experience something of daily life living alongside one of its families.

The village of Tujereng had expanded along a grid of sandy tracks spreading out from a central open square at its northern end. The square was dominated by the double minareted white mosque and an ancient, gnarled tree. Green melons were piled against the trunk of the tree and sold by the slice on trestle stalls set up under its branches. This place formed the meeting point for gossip, people watching, and rides by taxi and minibus to the market in Tanji by the coast. Through the sandy thoroughfares, children played, dogs roamed, and women sold home cooked snacks on their doorsteps. In the evenings the cows wandered by, prodded and pushed by stick waving herders. Here, young children cheekily shouted, 'white one' and confidently ran up to me with open hands to make contact and initiate play.

Tujereng's gradual expansion had been controlled by an elected association of villagers and chaired by one of their revered elders. Development projects were managed and funded with due attention to the recommendations of the villagers and these representatives. Saikhu was the social secretary and a central figure in galvanising fundraising and action amongst the villagers. He proudly showed me the latest project of a medical centre to be built on the land that the village was given for that very purpose. The foundations had been dug by hand and a pile of bricks were stacked in a corner ready for its outer walls. Saikhu excitedly waved a drawing of the site plan whilst staking out the plot, describing the vision of the clinic, the location of the nursing rooms, its health checks area, and the store. The next stage would depend on getting together a crew of willing builders and helpers.

Unperturbed by how long these projects take to complete, Saikhu showed me the ones that were fully operable. We entered the lively courtyard of the village's nursery school and were shown into the headteacher's office. The headteacher, Fatou Jobe, lay on her side on a thin mattress on the floor of her office breastfeeding her baby boy under her wrap whilst conducting her senior team meeting. The team halted their conversation to greet us and hands were touched around the group. As it was breaktime, we strolled around the school to meet the children and staff. Singing broke out in the open-air dining area where a teacher stood on one of the table dividers, controlling the numbers of blue uniformed young students. As the cooks prepared trays of rice and stew, groups of eight students squatted on the floor and huddled around the tin trays. The students took handfuls of food, rolling each one into a ball with their fingers before popping it expertly into their mouths. They were exuberant, freely expressing their vitality as we passed amongst them.

The government-run primary school was located on the main road by the coast. This large concrete yellow and brown compound overflowed with students and operated two daily shifts to provide education to over 1,100 students. We found the headteacher, Jarra Bittaye, and deputy headteacher, Kumbo Jawo, in their office. These two experienced leaders emanated strength and competence. They calmly navigated the complexities of running this large organisation with limited funds and a dependency on their local community. Saikhu introduced me to the teachers who were taking their break at the back of the courtyard in the shade. The teachers sat on concrete blocks around a small open fire upon which a pot of water boiled for a waiting teapot. They greeted us curiously and asked Saikhu for updates on the project involving the renovation of the water tanks. In the courtyard we met Fatima and her vendor friends who had come from the village to sell snacks and ice lollies to the students at break time. Their enterprising exchange clearly suited both the vendors and the customers.

Whilst supervising the students playing around the veranda of the L-shaped building, a teacher updated Saikhu on the latest teacher visit. Each year two staff members are seconded from school in Luxembourg, where Baku and his wife are employed, to work alongside the staff here. The reviews of their visit were very positive. Not only had they learnt how to teach large classes with few resources, but they had also engaged in partnership teaching, which stretched their expertise and challenged their perspectives to new interpretations and realities. Next year, two teachers will be seconded to school in Luxembourg and reciprocate the experience.

Back in the shade of the compound, I squatted next to Fatima to start descaling the fresh fish for dinner. Saikhu sat close by and offered more details on the village projects; he was optimistic that once the clinic was completed, work could begin to tarmac some of the sandy tracks. He hoped that the government would help but was concerned that this might not be enough.

"We have to help ourselves; we cannot rely on our government or the occasional generous handout from foreigners. It is always going to be a slow process and using all our skills and willpower. We will go one brick at a time." Saikhu smiled as he got up and stretched. He walked off with his dog at his heels to pick jackfruit from the trees in the compound.

5 – SOUTHERN SENEGAL

THE IMPROMPTU FESTIVAL

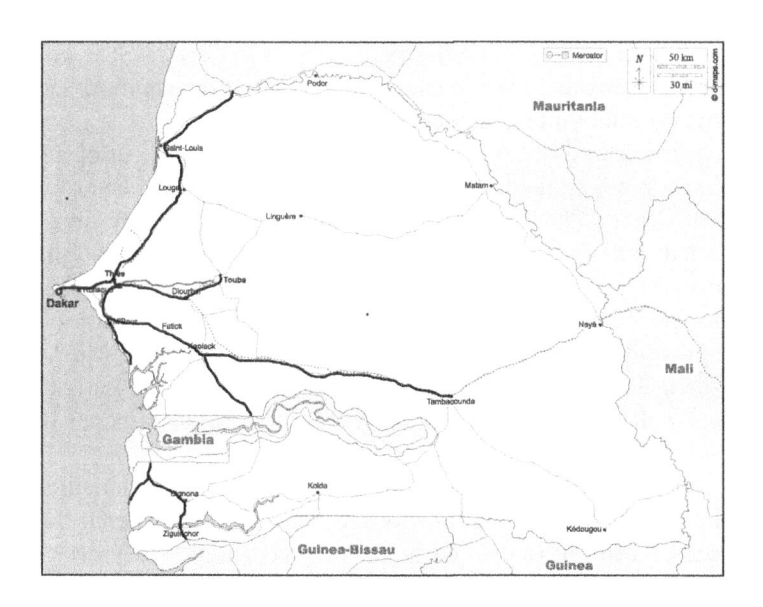

The hypnotic rhythm of the drums welcomed us. We could hear it intensify as we got closer; the snakes of sound chasing each other in a frenetic interwoven ensemble, both summoning and enticing. The cacophony of vibrations echoed around my head as I collected my luggage from the top of the shared taxi. I had not anticipated this kind of energy in such a small, dreamy fishing village situated beside the Atlantic.

I asked the young driver of a motorcycle taxi for a ride to the address I had on a piece of paper pulled from my pocket. Banku Mussa, the house of the earth mother, had been recommended to me by two German women I'd met in Mbour, a city further north. They had given me only a few details, but the resonating assurance that this would be an unforgettable experience. By motorbike we weaved through the sandy backroads of the village and pulled up beside a life-sized laughing sculpture of a vibrantly dressed local woman balancing a pot ringed with cowry shells on her head. The art piece provoked humour and I was still smiling when its crafter answered the echoing bell ring. Though unannounced, my arrival at Regula's gate was met with friendly ease and openness and she led me into the inner sanctuary of her home.

The sound of the djembe drums drifted in and out of my head as we walked through the cool chambers of her property. The walls, matching the colour of the soil, were decorated with shells and hummed with the gentle breath of its evocative paintings and flowing textiles. As if exposing her inner most secrets, Regula humbly shared the inspiration and concept behind each detail. The name 'Banku Mussa' seemed strangely underrated for a place steeped in creativity and spirituality, set deep in this rural corner of Casamance in southwest Senegal.

I was offered the blue room overlooking the bougainvillea bushes and a glittering effigy of a mosaic covered cockerel. The room's calm hues exuded peace and security. I slowly began to ease myself into the family of other guests, embracing this temporary inclusion, sense of home and nurturing cocoon.

An escalation of drumming celebrated the fading of the sun and began to unite in a professional profusion of riffs, each one layering and lifting the next into a mesmerising arousal, drowning all other sound. Scooters and running villagers sped along the track by the property's fence, drawn in by the beats and uplifting energy. The festival had begun.

Within the walls of Banku Mussa, a serene light flowed across the terrace from the faded electricity bulbs draped with bougainvillea flowers. Regula and her assistant, Ismeal, attentively prepared the meal for the six invited guests. We caught glimpses of their work through a shifting curtain separating us from the simple kitchen. Together they created courses of exquisite vegetarian food prepared with produce selected from the local market and crafted with the expertise of masters. As guests we were their audience, enveloped in a dance performance of servitude and pleasure.

In the sweet aftermath of delicious nourishment, we became a family, sharing stories and vulnerabilities. David, a customised tours' guide had brought his nieces on a trip from Spain. He had arranged to take them to meet the Diola people living in the remote villages close by so that they could learn first-hand some of the deep animistic traditions of this region. Oliver had travelled from Germany and was using this experience to extend his confidence as an adult with autism. Kasha and Musa were artists on their annual revisit from Poland where they lived. Kasha was perfecting her African dance technique, taking daily classes at the village community centre. Musa was a musician, booked to play the kora, a 21-stringed instrument, at the festival now in full party mode by the beach. He was restless and disappeared to the couple's room at the rear of the house, silently returning much later with his kora in hand. He settled into a bamboo chair in the shadows and began to play, resting the intricately decorated gourd on his thighs whilst his fingers flowed across the taut strings. His eyes were closed, focused intently on the creation of ancient melodies holding ancestral secrets. We silently witnessed Musa as he transcended to another space, sourcing lyrics and sounds that seemed to be performed for another audience far more reverent than us. It was spellbinding, one of those precious, priceless moments when life spontaneously unfolded as the company and ambience allowed. I noticed Ismeal in the corner, hugging Regula's dog that had stealthily crawled up into his lap. He watched Musa's fingers intently and added his own voice to softly sing words of love, loss and courage in unison. Regula pulled two of her signature finger puppets onto her slender hands. One had a mop of orange wiry hair and a blue gingham dress, the other a scalp covered in thick dreadlocks and a pair of long baggy shorts. The puppets' heads bobbed along to the music whilst Regula's hands worked their bodies into a wavering dance on the tabletop.

Musa eventually returned his attention to our little gathering under the thatched roof of Banka Mussa's terrace. We applauded, forever grateful for the magical festival that had just evolved in our midst.

6 – GUINEA-BISSAU

IN SEARCH OF CHIMPANZEES

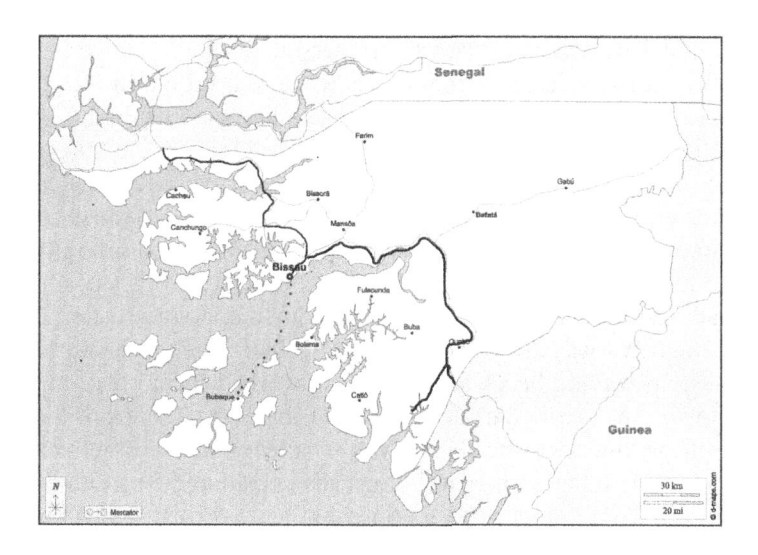

When you surrender to the deep flow of independent travel, spontaneous synchronicities can appear out of nowhere. A short unplanned conversation with a stranger can open the door to the next step of your journey. This was how I untangled the web of life in Guinea-Bassau and ended up tracking chimpanzees in the Cantanhez National Park, in the far southern corner of this tiny nation.

It started in central Bissau. Nico's enterprising development, Casa Cacheu, and Lina's family run sanctuary, Pension Creole, were guesthouses providing oases of homely comforts. These establishments brought together business visitors, travellers, and overseas employees of non-profit organisations. The simple rooms, shared facilities, and open patios blended restful tranquillity with communal exchanges. There

I learnt about the adventurous option for crossing the border into Guinea from Jemberem, a traditional village based in the rainforest in the most southern region, via motorbike. I met Helene, who was living in the village, one morning at Casa Cacheu. She was a research student from Switzerland and on her way to Europe for a long-anticipated family visit.

Helene was an extraordinary person. She had made it her life's purpose to discover as much as she could about the interlacing relationship of the Jemberem villagers with the forest that surrounded them. A long-term resident of the village and fluent in its Portuguese Creole dialect, Helene radiated the energy, attitude and habits of its people. She was the most knowledgeable and committed advocate for the community outside of their ethnic group, and she spread her respect and admiration to other researchers who lined up to intern alongside her. I was drawn into the magical intrigue of her world over pizza and beers, served at her favoured Italian bistro in town. The richly narrated stories of the characters from the village, the scientifically analysed challenges caused by freak weather changes, the psychologically considered frustrations rising from unmet expectations, and her deep respect for the villagers' mystical relationship with the forest, all submerged me in the intellectual universe of this superior being. I was hooked, absolutely determined to embrace her advice and experience this place for myself.

There was clearly no known schedule for the transport to Jemberem. At the bus station, I was told the bus sometimes left on Tuesdays and Thursdays before sunrise, dependent on the driver and the condition of the vehicle. Along with other passengers I chose a Tuesday to hang around the bus station with reserved anticipation, and by sunrise the old, battered bus rolled out of the station packed with passengers, packages, food produce and chickens, heading towards our destination. Seven hours later it slowed to swerve along a rutted earth-packed track surrounded on both sides by a tall dense forest. A passenger indicated that this was the beginning of the 1,000 square kilometre Cantanhez National Park, which spread without divisions across the landscape towards the border with Guinea. We had entered a timeless world; one seeped in traditions, rhythmically pulsating in harmony with the organic mass of surrounding foliage. The bus came to a stop next to a faded sign that had a barely decipherable map topped by a scratched painting of a chimpanzee's head. It heralded the name of the village, Jemberem, as the gateway to the biggest national park in Guinea-Bissau. The remaining innards of the bus were deposited in an open square by the roadside shacks selling basic household provisions. A group of whispering women observed us from a doorway whilst two oil-stained mechanics continued to examine a dismantled motorbike. All other signs of life were concealed inside the adobe walls within the compounds beyond.

Dazed and a little disorientated, I headed to one of the shops and asked for directions to the village hotel or inn, known as an auberge. A stern, rotund woman dressed in a tightly wound wrap led me through the labyrinth of immaculately swept courtyards that demarcated each homestead, and along padded earth pathways towards a cluster of round conical shaped buildings at the rear of the village that comprised the auberge. One of these huts became my home, complete with a torn mosquito net draped over a slightly damp mattress, a dry tap, a broken plastic bucket, and an electric light bulb that would emit a dim glow for a few hours each evening.

As the sun sank behind the dense web of the kapok trees, lianas and palms that encroached into the garden, the sounds of the village changed. The call to prayer echoed across the village and the slip-slap of passing flip flops faded towards the direction of the mosque. The final call seemed to signal the start of rhythmic thuds that came from each direction around my hut. Peering into the darkness, I could see the flames of open fires and in their shadows the moving figures of women pounding foo-foo, a dough made from cassava, in wooden mortars with thick cylindrical pestles. The sound announced the imminent arrival of food and beckoned families back to their compounds for the end of another day.

Mamadu arrived on my doorstep that evening. He had received a message from Helene asking him to take me into the forest to track chimpanzees. Helene had omitted to tell me that she also trained the park rangers and Mamadu was their leader. As always, the communication chain in African society surprised me; knowing that one person automatically links you to a network of others and before you have had time to plan your itinerary, the right people have been lined up to guide you. Helene had waved her wand from afar and Mamadu agreed to meet me early the next morning.

So as the sun started to rise and the village began to stir, Mamuda and I set off towards the main track that would lead us into the dense forest, now coming alive with bird song. Smoke from the compound fires curled into the morning mist as we greeted the early risers returning from the river with water containers balanced with ease on their heads. Mamuda checked his phone for tracking information posted by other rangers tagging the movements of the main chimpanzee troupe. Somewhere in distance the colobus monkeys were hollering, and the bird chorus intensified.

We were crouched in the undergrowth, peering across a gap in the forest and straining our eyes towards the distant tree line when the large female chimpanzee came into view. She held onto a branch with one arm and her baby with the other, her mouth chomping on a bunch of plucked leaves as she surveyed the treetops. We waited, hoping to catch a glimpse of others, until she moved along a branch and disappeared into the depth of the forest where the males were calling. This sighting seemed almost staged, a beautiful example of an undisturbed ecosystem allowing a nursing chimpanzee to have a moment of peace before joining the troupe. I felt like I had intruded into a secret world protected by some kind of spiritual boundary that Mamuda and I could never cross.

This feeling of otherworldliness descended again as we tiptoed along a track sticking close to the bushes. We crept forwards to a spot in the track where Mamadu knew the troupe would sometimes cross. He'd had a tipoff from a ranger that the troupe were shifting in our direction, slowly eating their way westwards to their sleeping area. We kept low and squatted, listening closely to every undergrowth crackle and shrill bird call. When Mamadu drew a sharp breath and grabbed my shoulder, I knew they were getting close. The male came first, striding ahead down the track with his rear end swaying and his eyes alert. He took off into the tangle of lianas just metres from us, followed by darting youngsters and a squabbling row of females carrying their young. The unruly procession dispersed into the undergrowth and separated into the trees, their deep calls resounding across the valley.

Returning to the village it was hard to believe this scene had been real and that this troupe lived so close to the village hub of humanity. I started to realise the fragility of this relationship; the delicacy of trying to maintain the fine balance between traditions, development and survival. Helene's unbounded commitment in understanding and preserving this interdependency now made more sense.

7 – GUINEA

FAST FADING MEMORIES OF YESTERYEARS

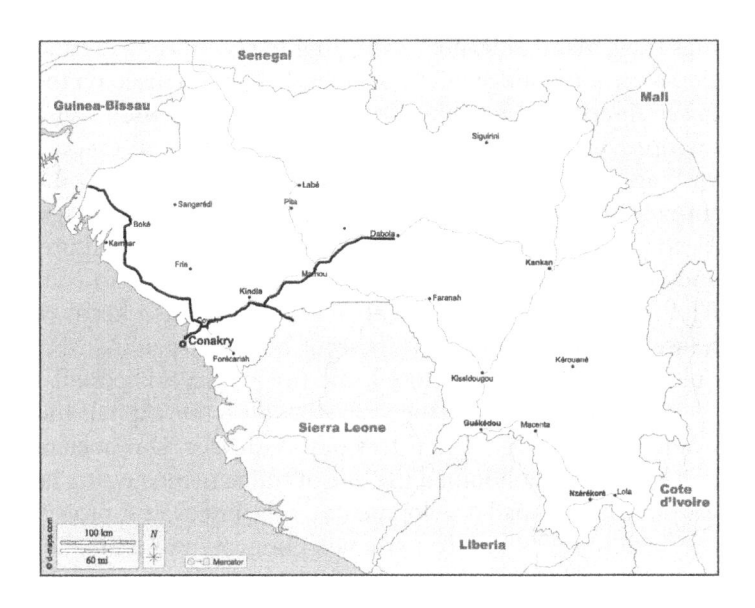

"In days past, French colonialists would take any opportunity they could to leave sweaty Conakry behind and decamp to the cool, clear climes of the delightful hill town of Dabola." These evocative words in the guidebook conjured up visions of serene, peaceful hotels, white linen tablecloths, and cocktails served on terraces with views overlooking rolling green hills, forest-filled valleys and gushing waterfalls.

These images belonged to the colonial French rule which ended in 1958. Since then, Guinea has been beset by 65 years of political, economic and social unrest including violent clashes between leading parties, an Ebola outbreak, and the most recent Covid pandemic. The future of the country was still uncertain during the time of my visit; it was being led by an interim military government and imminent elections were provoking emotionally charged discussions.

The Bambeto bus station had defiantly retained its location in the undignified backyard of the ever-expanding northern suburbs of Conakry. Its crumbling colonial buildings staggered and leaned, struggling to stay upright around the storerooms and small businesses that were housed on the lower floors. The balconies fronting the cheap rooms and cramped bars on the first floor were buckled and cracked with age. Down below, the shared taxis lined up under the tin-roofed stands, the foremost ones piled high with bags, plastic containers, food produce, small items of furniture, and the occasional motorbike. Men were employed to configure convoluted arrangements that secured these heaps of household belongings onto the roof before tarpaulins were pulled tight, doors were closed, and tire pressures checked.

We pulled out into the backstreets of the capital and headed towards the main artery out to the east. Our ancient and loaded Renault joined the line of traffic manoeuvring its way around the road developments on the highway. A project overseen by a Chinese construction company was issuing in the new era of dual carriageways and smooth cambers. In the meantime, the population struggled through diversions clouded in red dust. It was only once we started our ascent into the mountainous region of Fouta Djallon that the air began to clear, and the views of forests and valleys emerged. We overtook heavy trucks on their way to Mali, slowly hauling their loads up and around the curves of this stretch of newly tarmacked road. Some vehicles had become casualties of strain and age, pulled over to the side with makeshift brushwood warning signs urging other drivers to give them space. The drivers would crouch within the engines or rest from exertion in the shade under the axles.

The road from Mamou to Dabola began to herald a calmer, cleaner and more peaceful ambience. Small homesteads were scattered along the roadside, delicately concealed behind flowering magnolia and jasmine. At strategic bends in the road, enterprising villagers sold homegrown vegetables, carved wooden stakes and hand-crafted three-legged stools to passing trade. We had clearly entered a more fertile land of market gardens and spacious compounds.

Dabola sprawled along a grid of roads arranged over a cluster of small hills. Clinging to the back of a motorbike taxi I rode out of town on one of these thoroughfares, heading for Hotel SIB. The long sweeping drive led to the hotel's small entryway, which opened into the artistically decorated hallway and empty spacious dining area. These once elegant rooms now housed a large screen showing the latest World Cup Football replays, competing with Afrobeat music blaring from speakers out in the grounds. The tended lawns, flower beds and swimming pool proudly maintained their stance on terraces above a bar area hosting groups of teenagers visiting from the town.

In search of the promised tranquillity of this hill station, I spent the rest of my stay as the only guest at a simple auberge close to town. At the restaurant next door, I ate delicious fish and rice and joined other spectators to see the high school's football team beat their rivals.

The town's tourist centre was overgrown and abandoned by its supporting founders. In the past, the office arranged local guides to accompany visitors on hikes around the countryside. These activities had now become the luxury of the occasional adventurous expat from Conakry or a tailor-made travel group. Undeterred, I set off to discover the route to Pont de Dieu, a series of waterfalls that passed under a natural rock bridge. The rough pathway promised access to cultivated farmland and scattered villages and could have provided the perfect day's hike if it had not been for the gang of young boys who stood in my way. Their ringleader shouted disconnected words in French demanding the necessity to have them as my guides for my own safety for an unreasonable payment upfront. I was taken aback by their persistence and irritated at their intimidating tactics. No amount of arguing, explaining or ignoring worked. Defeated, I stamped angrily back up the path to the main road.

Alisan was pouring petrol into the tank of his motorbike through a hose attached to a plastic container. He offered to take me to Pont de Dieu and laughed when I told him of the boys' antics. "They're used to rich tourists who give them lots of presents – they'll always try it on with someone with a white face." His explanation lightened my mood and we set off, bumping along the same track, past the houses where the boys had now disappeared and on into the valley alongside the cabbage fields and rice paddies. The track became narrower and criss-crossed with tree roots as we headed into the dense forest. Alisan slowly negotiated the motorbike through the foliage and down into the valley. We came to a halt at the sound of rushing water and hopped off the bike, scrambling over rocks to get a glimpse of the first waterfall. As promised, these waterfalls cascaded under a rock formation down to the cultivated valley below. Alisan spoke to a young boy who had appeared silently from further down the track. He led us over the natural rocky bridge to a crack in the wall of granite on the other side of the waterfall. Pointing into the shadows, he directed our eyes towards a large python that was slithering its way down between the boulders. I tensed and stared silently, fascinated by this huge reptile moving away thankfully at a safe distance from us.

Dabola proved to be a town full of surprises, adventures and challenged expectations. It took time and patience to find the information, guidance and tranquillity once cherished by yesteryear visitors from the city. Nevertheless, this area of Guinea provided an opportunity to explore a fascinating part of the country where the memories and remnants of its colonial past were fast disappearing into the town's development. I was left wondering whether there would be a time in the future when the economic stability of the country would entice visitors to return to this district, and whether the new tarmacked road would help to make decamping to the hills a pleasurable possibility when the temperatures started to rise by the coast.

8 – SIERRA LEONE

HUNTING FOR THE ELUSIVE ELEPHANTS

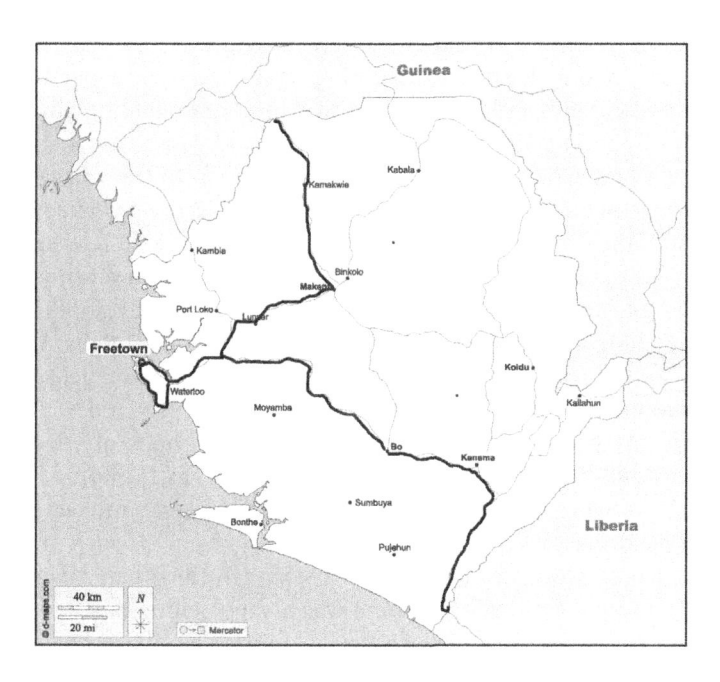

The only light making its way through the canvas of my tent was the faded glow of a crescent moon. And keeping the moon company was a spectacular coverage of stars sprinkled on every inch of the sky outside. I could have imagined a calming picture of the slow drop of a shooting star, the traverse of an intruding satellite or the changing silhouettes of the forest. Instead, I laid rigid in my sleeping bag listening intently to the cacophony of sounds around me; the deep screeches followed by responding cackles of the colobus monkeys, the hoots and shrill calls of settling birds, and the snuffles of small rodents in the undergrowth close by. The forest seemed more alive now than in full daylight or maybe it was just my imagination. Fully alert, I strained my ears to pick out any sound that could belong to the soft tread of a human footstep close to my tent.

I had arrived at the largest and most remote National Park in Sierra Leone on the back of a motorbike, riding 40 kilometres from the border crossing with Guinea. I had entered Sierra Leone legally by stepping over a chain suspended between poles and patiently waiting in a rundown hut whilst a policeman stamped my passport by hand. For a reasonable fee, I had arranged for a motorbike driver from the adjacent village of Sainya to take me to Koto village at the entrance to the National Park. The driver warned me that the route would be long and somewhat unpleasant. Despite the description, the journey turned out to be an intrepid adventure bouncing along dusty tracks rutted from use and past rainfalls. We passed through settlements occupied by the Susu people, where the village activities of cooking, washing, and water and firewood collecting were in full flow. Groups of young boys holding machetes and sticks, walking to the forest to hunt or work on their family's farmland, looked up and waved as we drove by.

Koto village was bigger and busier than the other villages we had passed through. There was a shop selling basic provisions, two loaded pickup trucks, and a few dust-covered motorbikes propped up on stands by the roadside. Villagers gathered under the big tree in the centre and on the verandas in front of the single-storey mud brick houses shaded by tin roof overhangs. We stopped outside the park's office to meet Ramadam, the young chief of the village and manager of the park. Ramadam was visibly flustered by my unexpected arrival, but proceeded to ask if I had a tent suitable for the terrain. I confirmed this and received permission to continue the ride along the path into the forest.

I was surprised to find the park devoid of occupation and any facilities. All the accommodation was in ruins or being slowly dismantled. Other than one park ranger, who greeted us as we drew into a clearing amongst the trees, there was no sign of tourism or life. This is where the motorbike driver left me with my rucksack. The ranger indicated where to pitch my tent and pointed towards the river where I could wash and get water. He helped me collect firewood and lent me a pot to boil water, then hung around whilst I put up my tent and asked about food. I felt vulnerable in his presence and wary of his intentions, though his interactions seemed helpful and friendly enough. The arrival of a pickup truck carrying five other visitors from Freetown eased my concerns and diverted the ranger's attention. I quickly befriended my new neighbours and later joined them for a dinner of fish and rice delivered from the village. We arranged a guided hike together in the morning towards the interior of the park with the hope of seeing hippos and elephants. I thanked the universe for sending some company and protection in this isolated spot.

The rise in temperature and crescendo of noise outside the tent heralded the rapid beginning of a new day. I had survived the night without being too disturbed. With relief I crawled out into the sunlight to a breakfast of omelette and bread delivered from the village. An older, experienced ranger, Cila, joined our group to lead our hike. He took us down to the riverside and arranged us into relays so we could take turns crossing the river in the only canoe. "Your elephant hunt begins here," he laughed as he pushed the canoe out of the shallows and started paddling across the flow of the river towards the other bank. I sat in the bow with three of the other visitors, keeping the balance between us. We scanned the banks for signs of hippos but were without luck. Instead, a troupe of colobus monkeys swung across the branches of the huge cotton trees ahead accompanied by calls from the boubou and whydah birds, native to this area.

Cila led us up the riverbank and across the grassland dotted with remarkable Disney-like termite castles and marked with potential tracks of duikers and bushpigs. We battled our way behind him through the head-high grasses, which scratched at our skin as we fought our way forwards. Ahead, our guide swung his machete at the brittle stems and cut a pathway for us. He came to an eventual stop before a huge cotton tree with a buttress of interwoven roots surrounded by kola trees. Beneath the canopy Cila started to share snippets of the history of this area. This was one of the gathering places for hunters who used to come to the park to track elephants as a sport. He talked of the mass export of their tusks and the illegal trafficking of other animal species to stock zoos and medical laboratories abroad. It was the park's founder, Geza Telaki, who worked with the Sierra Leone government to put an end to this lucrative business and establish this protected area in 1974. "The numbers of elephants have dwindled over the years, the herds only come near the villagers when they are distressed and hungry. We leave them alone to live deep in the forest. Perhaps today we will see their tracks," Cila informed us.

We kept our eyes on the undergrowth, hunting for signs of elephant footprints, their dung or eating remnants, sadly without success. The elusive herds were clearly far from our tracks. We terminated our forage into this hostile undergrowth at an old ranger's hut called the Elephant Camp. Hidden in a scramble of thick tangled vines was the brick remains of a building, originally the concealed hive of the elephant hunters we were told. Nights and days would be spent here, awaiting the sighting of these sought-after creatures. We turned away from the park's sinister history and retraced our tracks across the savannah. I was quietly relieved that we had not seen any evidence of the elephants. Hopefully, they were far away from intrusive human contact, living deep in the forest and carefully protected by the local villagers and these committed park rangers.

Back at the camp site we settled in for a more relaxed dinner of fish and spaghetti, listening to the beating music coming from the village where Ramadam's wedding feast was taking place. Now fully integrated into the village, he was marrying one of the Koto women, a decision of commitment and loyalty to the Tambakha Chiefdom and the National Park's future. The distant Afrobeat seemed to merge naturally with the relentless trill of the forest's insects and the occasional hollering of the male primates calling in the distance.

9 – LIBERIA

RISING FROM THE WAVES OF TIME

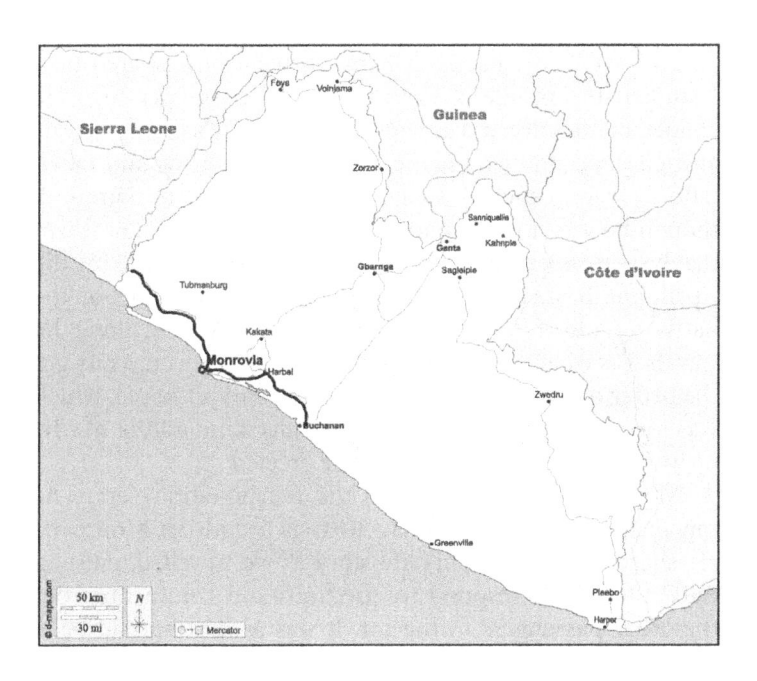

It's been 20 years since civil war ended in Liberia. Since then, a more stable period has been established across the country. At the time of my visit the population was awaiting the fourth general election in this post-war period, the first to be managed by Liberian authorities without international funding or assistance. The people I spoke to were hopeful for further stability and development for the country. They wished for the leadership that would continue to improve the economy, the fight against corruption, and the finalising of the remaining prosecutions of economic and war crimes.

The resulting elections in October and November 2023 led to a close win for Joseph Boakai, a former vice-president and leader of the Unity Party. The small marginal gain in votes saw the end to the term of office for President George Weah of the Coalition of the Democratic Change Party. The rebuilding of the nation was about to enter its third decade.

As I sat in the back left-hand corner of the shared taxi, I studied the profile of the man in the passenger seat. He exuded confidence and greeted the police and security guards at each checkpoint by name. His muscular arms and faded tattoos were exposed suggesting a military background, though he was unarmed and in civilian clothes. I later learnt that he was a member of the Kpelle ethnic group, speaking the Kpelle and Bassa languages interchangeably depending on the native tongue of the officers and the people we met along the way. It was when he slipped into English that my curiosity got the better of me. I introduced myself, learnt his name, which was Morris Matadi, and started to understand a little of why he was revered by many of those he greeted.

Morris was travelling from the rehabilitation centre he ran in the town of Buchanan to visit friends in Monrovia. He shared snippets of his life story as we travelled, pausing intermittently to respond to questions and comments from the other passengers in the car. It was as if a tap had been turned and out was pouring a biography of incredible tragedy, courage and opportunity.

The narrative started from an event in 1990 when he was eleven years old, which was to change his destiny. On this day, Morris told us, he had lost his parents and siblings at the infamous rebel checkpoint on the outskirts of Monrovia called 'God Bless You Gate'. After a month of trying to survive on his own he, like many other orphaned young people, found himself enlisted into the rebel army fighting against the militia government lead by Sergeant-President Samual Doe. In 1997, he became embroiled as one of the key members of Charles Taylor's army in the early days of the warlord's regime. It was then that he knew he had to get away. Risking his life, he journeyed overland via the Côte D'Ivoire to the Buduburam refugee camp in Ghana. Morris described the confusion that reined in the camps. He was continually encouraged to join the rebel groups in other west African countries, whilst being rebuked daily by other fleeing refugees for the part he had played in the devastation on civilians back in his home country. He described the experience as 'hellish'.

He talked on, explaining how a group of refugees banded together to refuse this recruitment process and reached out to United Nations workers for support. Until 2003, when the civil war ended in Liberia, UNHR funding and resources were made available in the Ghana-based camp so that young ex-soldiers could have access to counselling, advice and skills training. Morris says he was one of the lucky ones, his training helped him become strong again and start to believe he had a future. He decided he had to share what he had learnt in Ghana with other ex-soldiers still living in Liberia.

As we pulled into the motor park at Buchanan junction on the outskirts of Monrovia, adults and children began to crowd around our vehicle touting for business, desperate for a few dollars in exchange for carrying luggage, taking messages for a driver, or selling a few trinkets such as cigarette lighters and plastic dolls. There was a frenzy of attention-grabbing mania as people vied for passengers' interest and the chance to make some money.

Morris, I noticed, attracted a different kind of attention. A group of men congregated around him, offering embraces, friendly banter, and humourous exchanges. In response, Morris calmly drew them nearer to check how they were. They exchanged warm greetings with me too. I noticed that each one held some kind of support crutch that helped them manoeuvre between the vehicles, their amputated legs concealed within a knotted jogging pant leg or exposed beneath sagging shorts. Those with amputated arms bent them at the crook of the elbow or let them dangle beneath the sleeve of a T-shirt. I could not help but notice the rough rutted scar tissue running across the stumps.

In a quiet corner of the motor park, Morris wrote down the links to videos, articles and contacts related to the foundation he had set up in Liberia upon his return. Based in Buchanan town, he had managed to commandeer a building from where he and a team of friends had provided rehabilitation programmes for other ex-soldiers like himself. Young men and women had come for support and training, they were encouraged to talk about and share their experiences, and to learn skills that could help earn an income and integrate into society. He had used some charity and government funding to provide education for orphaned children, arrange agricultural training and some land for the adults to work on, and start an education provision for the children of ex-soldiers who were struggling to stay in school and away from drugs and crime. He shared the latest short videos of the centre with me before we parted.

I later discovered how Morris's work had caught the attention of international investors. A charity based in the United States ran a storyline similar to the one I'd heard in the taxi, arousing interest and donations to help fund a week-long trip for Morris to attend training with other entrepreneurs in Colorado. Throughout those early years of stability within Liberia, he had gained some government-directed funding grants and charity sponsorships from Sweden, Germany, the United States, and the United Kingdom. These trickles of money and well-wishes had enabled him to pay the rental on the buildings, salaries of the teachers and psychologists, uniforms and schoolbooks for teachers and students, and pay the rent on land that could be used for the agricultural training programmes.

When I saw Morris again a week later, it was in a cramped restaurant building opening into the Buchanan motor park junction. The space smelled of the previous night's oily chicken grills merged with the fumes from the melted fat popping in the woks, ready for sweet balls of dough to be dropped in. He accepted a strong coffee, heaped in a medley of sugar, and began to slurp the thick liquid in between mouthfuls of fresh donut. The visit to Monrovia had gone well and he was ready to get back to work.

The next decade would look different for initiatives such as Morris's. The grants and sponsorships had dried up despite the team's advocacy, lobbying and fundraising efforts. Morris blamed this not only on the economic struggles of his country but on the change in the global foci. He had seen the Ebola and Covid outbreaks stall the number of visitors and NGOs coming to Liberia, the very people that he had connected with to seek funding for his foundation. He did not seem enthusiastic about any immediate changes following the upcoming elections either. "Now we are funding the foundation ourselves, through family donations and small bank loans." We competed with the outside noise from passing travellers, hawkers and vehicles, as Morris shared with me the financial overviews of the foundation's running costs that included rentals, yearly book orders, teachers' salaries, and furniture replacements. His bravado softened and the truth of his challenges started to spill out.

"We must keep on. I managed to get some money to pay for five uniforms for the third graders who don't have any – they need to be in uniform to take their exams. We now need to find a psychologist as our teachers need psychiatric support for themselves. They deal with some very difficult behaviour and reactions from students and adults every day. The experiences people have lived with have affected their minds. We need to stop this from affecting the next generation. My teachers don't know how to manage the behaviour of the youths in their classes." He then asked if I had any techniques to share with him.

We agreed to stay in touch and Morris stood up to leave. As we waved goodbye one of his friends joined him by the doorway, resting his arm across Morris's broad shoulders and hopping alongside as they made their way towards the shared taxi heading back to Buchanan. I watched them go, grateful for Morris's generous storytelling and inspired by his impactful work. I was left with much to consider alongside Morris's parting words: "It is changing what happens inside the mind that will help to build the future of Liberia."

10 – CÔTE D'IVOIRE

WATCHING BASKING SACRED CROCODILES

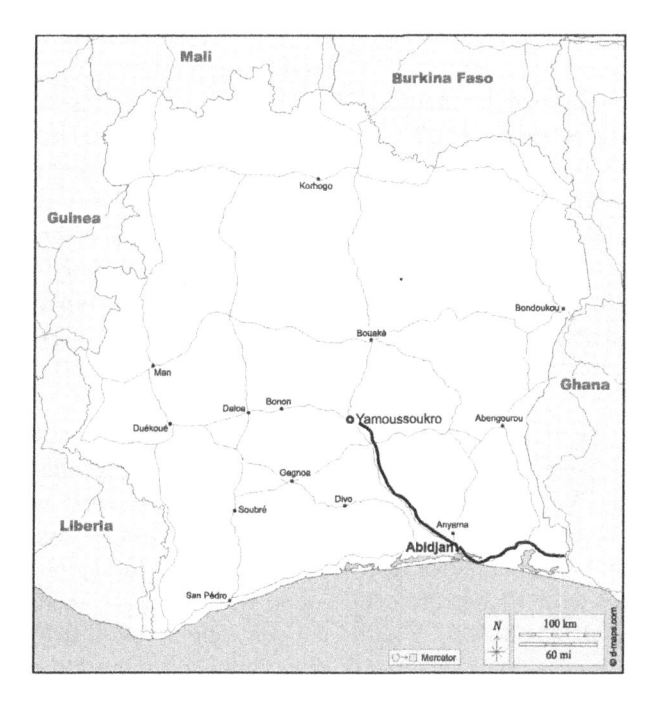

On the southern side of the presidential palace site in the capital city, Yamoussoukro, there is a lake occupied by sacred crocodiles. This information created a vision in my mind of some kind of sacred ritual ground from where onlookers could observe these reptiles. It was enough incentive to fuel a trip from the capital city of Abidjan to see them for real.

I was staying in Abidjan in the squeaky clean and increasingly modernised district of Le Plateau. Heavy plant machinery had brought new thoroughfares, riverside promenades and manicured roundabouts to the expanding metropolis. In this area there was a French-style café adjacent to a Chinese casino. Both were overlooked by the abandoned Brutalist-style La Pyramide, designed by the Italian architect Rinaldo Olivieri and completed in 1973. Abidjan was a mishmash of development and serenity. The city's older but vibrant heart was still evident, squeezed into the gaps and crumbling buildings standing proudly amongst its streets.

I welcomed the change of scenery at the Adjamé bus station, with its rutted muddy lanes and endless lines of traffic. Vendors selling their wares on the move and the dense sound of lively humanity all pushed against each other. The security round the bus station was visible, men moved towards me in labelled jackets indicating their right to guide me into the covered waiting area by the UTB ticket office. I bought a ticket from a dark booth inside the building and waited patiently, watching boxes of Spanish red wine and crates of South African apples being loaded into the undercarriage of the idling bus.

Yamoussoukro was a three-hour journey away, heading north-west from Abidjan and set amongst rolling hills and plains. We travelled on a straight tarmacked road where entrances to palm oil, rubber and banana plantations veered off on either side. Scattered villages, their buildings of mud bricks with thatch or metal roofs, were set back from the road. On the bus, a TV showed a continuous roll of two programmes: a comedy show of relentless shouting and hitting that drew laughter from the passengers, followed by a documentary about Niger that provided a head lolling interlude. The bus pulled into a gated bus station, and we all piled out into the sunshine.

I did not get to see the crocodiles straightaway as my taxi driver insisted that I first visit the Basilica. He said the main reason to visit the town should be to marvel at the splendour of this structure, which dominated the skyline and was shrouded in dust. I yielded to his enthusiasm and was driven to the entrance. The building filled the space on the northern side of the town, a strangely indulgent occupancy spreading its lavish veneer. I climbed the marble steps and entered a cavernous pew-lined space, dwarfed beneath the domed ceiling, towering pink Italian marbled pillars, shimmering chandeliers and the 7,000 square meters of stained glass. The opulence was intimidating, its flamboyant pride incredulous.

What had inspired the former president, Félix Houphouet-Boigny, to enlist the famous Lebanese architect Pierre Fakhoury to construct this incredible replica? How much did it cost to build? What purpose did this building serve? These questions whirled in my head as I wound my way up the spiralling staircase to the upper floor veranda to take in the view of the town below.

Back down on the ground I made my way over to the main attraction. The crocodiles were lounging in a man-made lake prominently located at the entrance to the lavish, gated presidential palace where Félix Houphouet-Boigny was buried. A crowd of onlookers marked the location of the crocodiles at a vantage spot beside the main road. Leaning over the low concrete wall, we could all get a clear view of the patterned bodies and yawning jaws. There was something quite mesmerising about watching these static reptiles absorb the late heat from the sun, which had managed to penetrate the dust ladened air. The crocodiles lay rigid, eyes unblinking, bodies unflinching and seemingly without breath. We stood observing in silence, watching for any sign that these motionless creatures would break their composure and dive into the water or turn to face us. Instead, their poise was broken only briefly if a neighbour turned and snapped its jaw. The stillness would quickly resume, penetrating the atmosphere around the lake edge. The gathering of visitors, locals and homeward-bound school students continued to watch, captivated.

Eventually, the stillness broke and a group of students talked in whispers recounting their day. I asked if they stopped here each afternoon. The tallest grinned and spoke for the group. "Who wouldn't –not every town has sacred crocodiles like this."

I later learnt that the term 'sacred crocodile' was the name given to the specific species of crocodile found in West Africa and was only identified as having distinct differences from the related Nile crocodile in recent years. These reptiles are known to have a shorter muzzle and overall length and are most frequently found basking in brackish waters in bright sunshine. It was clear that although there was no evidence of any ceremonial rituals, these animals were respected and protected here in Yamoussoukro. Their presence provided a quiet moment of contemplation for their curious observers.

11 - GHANA

THE DREAMER'S COCOON

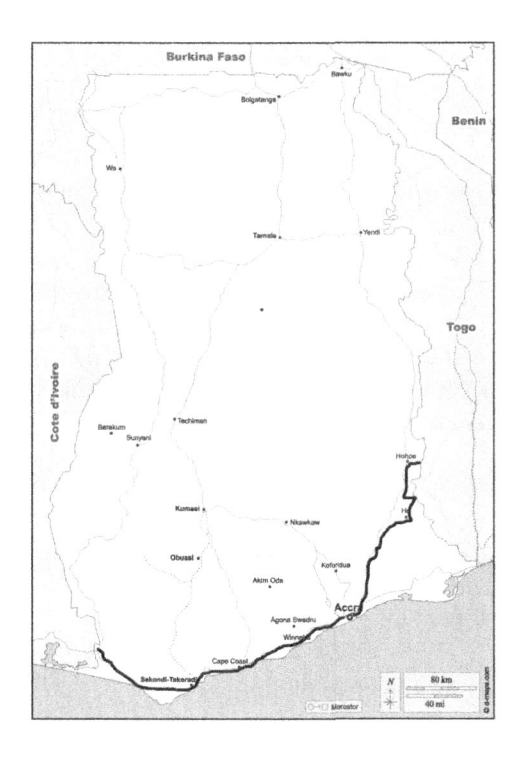

Life seemed to stall amongst the compounds wedged on land directly north of where Ring Road East meets Liberation Road. Most compounds were awaiting either negotiated development projects or demolition firms. Walking amongst them it was difficult to find the Institute Museum of Ghana. Its distinctive arched gateway and entrance were concealed behind an abandoned pharmaceutical company building and a pile of wooded pallets. I knocked on the large solid metal door bearing the institute's signage and heard its echo disappear into the cavernous space beyond.

The door was eventually opened by the curator, Sally. She led me into a light, spacious warehouse, minimal in its content apart from an assortment of displays arranged around its walls. There was a distinct smell of rubber and oil paint evoking memories of car repair shops. I had been taken straight into one of the exhibition spaces where Sally now offered to show me round.

Most of Dela Anyah's work hung from deeply drilled screws on the white walls of the warehouse. The installations were various interpretations constructed from upcycled strips of rubber bike tyre inner tubes and straps of treaded truck tyres. They were interwoven and arranged in such a way to produce powerful, textured forms secured with metal studs. A three-sided screen had been positioned in the centre in which you could stand, surrounded by the rubbery panels, for a moment of isolated contemplation.

> 'The moments of isolation
> Growing, nurturing, transforming
> Windows closed, curtains drawn
> Alone with one thought
> Alone with God
>
> Yearning for the birth of our new self
> And the death of our past self
> Days go and months come
> The dreams incubate, joy steadily rises
> Awaiting the day we tear open our cocoons
> And fly out as beautiful butterflies.'

Sally paused as I read Dela's words and then offered additional information. "Dela gets his inspiration from bicycle repair shops and vulcanisers in the city. Through his work, he aims to question the ideas of beauty, capitalism and environmental degradation."

She took me to an outside courtyard where streams of coloured fabric flowed down from the first-floor balcony and shimmered against the whitewashed walls. Doors opened into the courtyard from each side, and we entered one towards the back. In this space, the light was softer and the exhibition pieces smaller and more delicate. Intricately cut pieces had been selected from photographs of portraits and then layered to create distorted images arranged into slightly tarnished collages. You were required to come closer and look carefully, then revisit and reexamine the elaborate compositions. Sally explained that the artist, Mobolaji Ogunrosoye, explores ideas around the distorted perception of women by using photographic images of West African women on the continent and the diaspora.

Other doors led into studio spaces occupied by the artists in residence, who laid their materials on trestle tables and hung unfinished canvases on the grey concrete walls. Vibrant colours, intriguing compositions and provocative interpretations flowed within these rooms. These immense studios offered the luxury of space and focus – an artist's dreamland.

The team working behind the scenes at the Institute Museum of Ghana were skilled professional young people intent on creating an ecosystem where emerging artists can grow and develop their practice. Backed by generous donations from national and international sources, this independent non-profit institute has been able to transform old warehouses into thriving, creative hubs. Sally had shown me the results of the annual Noldor Residency programme, where two artists with limited access to infrastructure and material resources were provided with the opportunity to practise in a dedicated studio space and retreat from the distractions of daily life.

The team were proud of the increasing number of supported artists expanding their practice and developing career paths within the global art scene. During the last three years, they pooled their resourcefulness and commitment to create an expanding network intent on enabling artists to tell their stories and interpretations in their unique ways. As Sally concluded our tour, she explained how important it was that her generation could tell a different story about Ghana. "We want to tell a story of integrated heritages, respect and inclusion. We want the global community to recognise Ghana for its vibrant culture and energy, its interrelated themes and emerging dichotomies. These are far richer than the current tourist generalisations of just beaches, food and drumming."

The visions of these young people were clearly metamorphosing within these renovated buildings on the outskirts of Accra. The sense of joy was tangible – dreams were incubating, creativity was flourishing, and new opportunities were emerging.

12 – TOGO

THE TOWERS OF TAMBERMA VALLEY

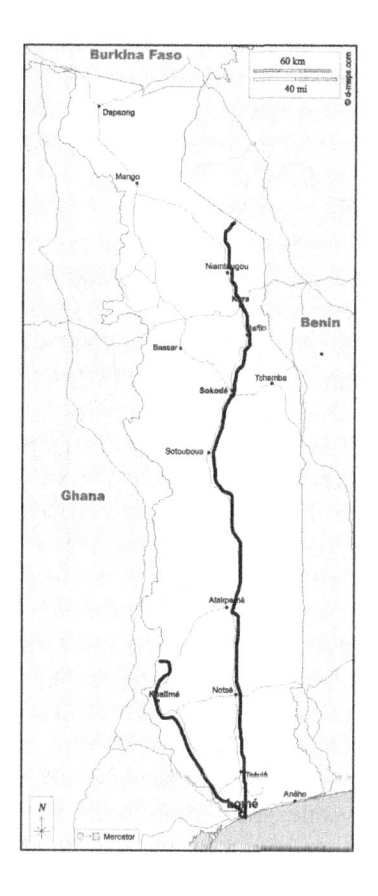

The head of the compound had deep, wise eyes that spoke to me despite our lack of a common language. These eyes had witnessed the changes and developments of his clan and people over his long life but had retained a soft curiosity and a mischievous twinkle. He sat next to me on a wooden platform wearing a red embroidered hat with a pointed tip and a thick woollen grey coat covering his thin lean chest. His faded jeans concealed his sinewy legs, which were stretched out in front of him. The jeans stopped at bare feet that showed years of contact with the earth. I told him my name and family story in short strands of French that were immediately translated into the Ditammari language by one of his sons. He nodded and smiled, shaking my hand and turning to make eye contact with his two wives who stood behind him. He gave nothing away. I would love to know what he really thought of tourists like me visiting his compound.

I had arrived by motorbike at Tamberma Valley in northern Togo after several hours of travel from the city of Kara. My driver, Baldin, was a student at the University of Kara studying science and working as a driver to pay his tuition fees. He spoke multiple languages including English and owned a reliable motorbike. We passed his university building on the way, one of the controversial investments brought to this remote town by a past Togo president, Gnassingbé Eyadéma (term 1967–2005). The ride took us along the empty tarmacked road that headed towards the northernmost region of the country and the border with Burkina Faso. The entry to Tamberma Valley was along a track of orange dust at a right hand turn in the village of Kande. We stopped at the junction to greet a few of Baldin's fellow university friends. They hitched a lift in a passing pickup truck and drove off ahead of us towards their family compounds in the valley.

There was an entry fee into the valley that also gave us permission to access one of the compounds. This compound had been open to visitors since 2004 as part of a UNESCO World Heritage project. My introduction to the head of this compound was the expected etiquette, as was donating money for the clan and purchasing some trinkets and vegetables from the women vendors. This process provided a small income to this specific clan who were all related in linage to the revered elder I had greeted. He remained sitting peacefully under the tree.

Baldin and I were invited into one of the homes, a tower-like structure with an entrance behind a number of mud brick altars covered with white splashes of paint and fetish objects. I stooped under a bundle of feathers tied above the doorway and entered a cool, dimly lit space. Animal droppings had been brushed to one side and there was a strong pungent smell of goat. In the corner was a smoke-lined alcove where pots and spoons were stacked next to charred logs under a hole open to the sky. A very narrow set of stairs, made from the same rust-coloured earth of the walls, led to a smoothly moulded roof top. From here we could see the layout of the village. There were several clusters of adjoining towers, thatched and metal roofed buildings, and an open space around which children played, goats roamed, and a gathering of women vendors were wrapping up their items into cloth bundles.

We crawled backwards into a small opening in one of the conical turrets to see the cool, dark sleeping area, which was safely hidden on the upper floor. Next to it was the grain store, accessed by a ladder with an internal drop that could contain a full harvest.

Back outside the entrance, Baldin showed me the altars where this family brought their offerings and prayers. There was an altar each for the harvest, prosperity, security and fertility. "The evil spirits are kept well away from this compound," he commented as we moved on.

On the edge of the compound, we looked across at the next cluster of towers nestled on a hillside surrounded by trees. The ground in between the two compounds had been cultivated and small sorghum bushes pushed through the earth next to potato plants. A young boy carefully guided a herd of goats around the open fields and up towards the village.

Along the track leading through the valley at the foot of the Atakora Mountains, more of these structures stood camouflaged against the earth and sparse vegetation. Each structure was different and bore the unique features of the clan that occupied it. I thought about the years of tradition that had shaped these forms and their family structures, the need for survival, self-sufficiency, and a reliance on nature.

13 – BENIN

TRAVEL PROTECTION FROM A VOODOO PRIEST

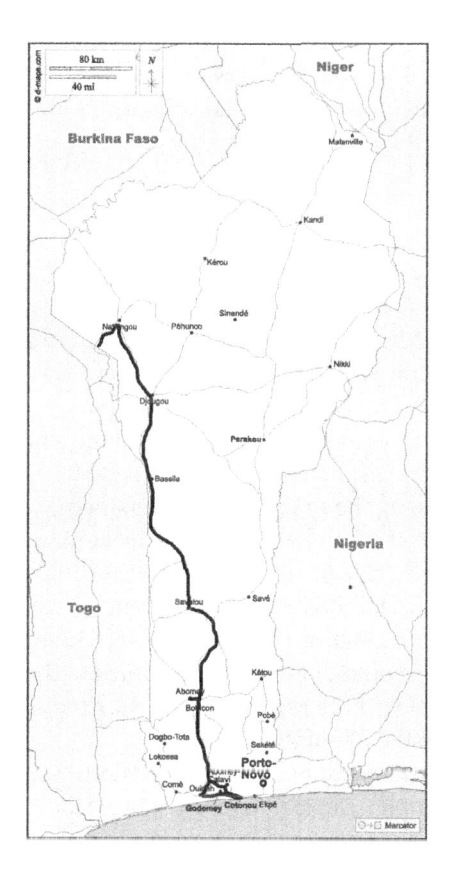

In the darkness of the room, I watched the priest reach amongst the assortment of dusty objects and select a rusty metal tin. He picked out a finger length piece of wood with a hole drilled through the middle of it. The wood had been sanded and carved with a simple geometric design. Around it was wrapped red string attached to a small wooden pin, which fitted into the hole exactly. He held the talisman over the head of one of the wooden statuettes in his collection and began to utter sounds and words that flowed into a chant-like song. With his other hand he scooped water from an open bowl and dripped it over the statuette's face, which seemed to look up to him in response. The priest then turned to acknowledge my presence and held the talisman out for me to take. "Place this around your neck on a necklace of string, it will keep you safe. You are protected now for your long journey."

Salano Akponkinto was one of many voodoo priests in this area who maintain the inherited traditions of his father and ancestors. He was small in stature, softly spoken and yawned frequently with fatigue. He said he had been performing several rituals out in the villages and had not slept much recently. As he squatted on the floor, he touched the rosary beads around his neck and flicked the front of his tunic top to rest over his matching cotton trousers.

This morning, he greeted my companion Sylvian and me at the door to the voodoo temple in his family village on the outskirts of the city of Abomey-Calavi in Benin. The village lay beyond the famous palaces and temples of the city that once was the capital of the Kingdom of Dahomey and had withstood the colonial powers for centuries. The ancient religious practice with its mythical, animist rituals continued to be integral to the life of the people.

Salano performed a cleansing ceremony before we could enter the temple. Armed with a coloured beaded rattle, he crouched outside the doorway knocking a rounded stone rhythmically on the step whilst chanting words to the supreme god. When satisfied we were not accompanied by bad spirits, we were welcomed into a darkened room where a cluster of old wooden figures stood amongst sand-covered stones, shells and small calabash bowls. On the earth wall behind them was the black outline of a hand-drawn leopard. Salano squatted on a low stool and brought a metal bowl of water close to his bare feet. He scooped water into his mouth and then proceeded to spit it out over the wooden figures, followed by chants. He asked the gods to intervene on behalf of Sylvian and myself as a preparation for our requests for help and support in our lives.

Outside the temple Salano performed a morning ritual to the gods of the rain and harvest. He talked to the collection of small erect wooden statues as if they were friends, gently touching them with the back of his hand, placing drops of water on their heads, and then completing the ceremony by spitting a shower of water over them all.

Back inside the temple, chickens wandered amongst us as we were shown the collection of medicinal objects used for healing and warding off bad omens. Next to other wooden statuettes marked with white paint and red powder were a collection of bottles containing the remains of palm wine and Fanta. There were numerous small bags of rocks and shells clustered next to a pile of fluffy feathers, a ram's horn and an old battery-operated radio. It was hard to tell how long these items had been here and whether the array was ever altered. Nevertheless, Salano described how he used combinations of some of the items to prepare medicines for his visitors and for the talisman that I had been given.

We bid goodbye and made our way along the village earth pathways to the main shrine used by the villagers for sacrifices to the supreme god or to one of the many deities. The concrete shelter of the shrine was located under a prominent tree whose lower bark was covered with inserted sticks. Bunches of feathers had been threaded onto twines strung around the trunk. Inside the shelter was the sacred moulded earth form of the god, fronted by a pile of sacrificial remains. Hungry goats munched debris amidst the pungent smelling heap that consisted of a decaying collection of chicken carcasses, melon skins and food offerings covered in yellow powder, drops of alcohol and white feathers.

I touched the talisman now tied around my neck and hoped that it would bring me protection for my onward trip. I certainly felt honoured to receive such a simple mystical and traditional token of the voodoo religion.

14 – NIGERIA

FROM A PIECE OF WHITE CLOTH

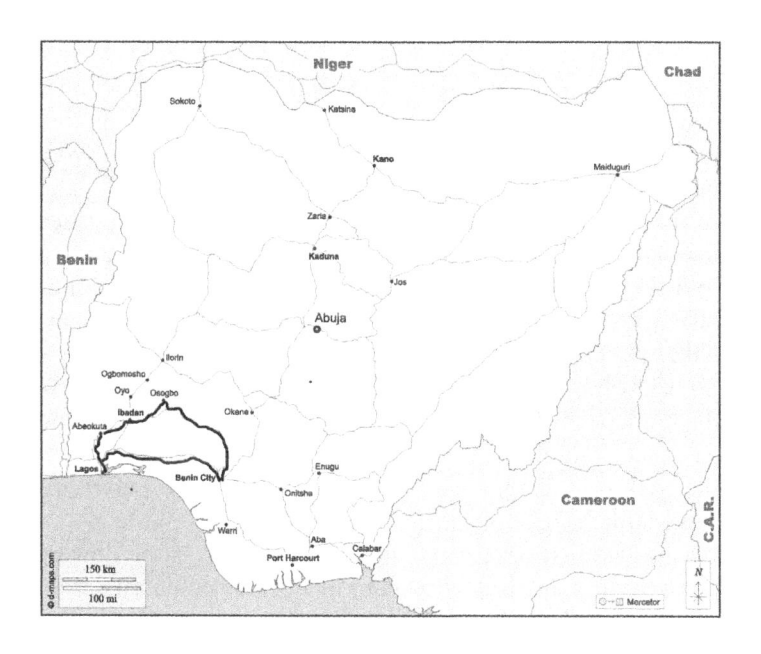

The city of Oshogbo guarded its rich knowledge of art traditions with secretive pride. Access to this university of expertise was akin to earning entrance to a sacred shrine; it involves human connection, earned trust and open curiosity.

The motorbike driver sped along the main road out of town. From over his shoulder, I scoured each building we passed for signs of the art gallery. Set back from the road it stood out because of the eclectic assortment of wooden sculptures propped up against its fragile facade.

Inside the gallery building streaks of sunlight managed to push through closed shutters to reveal a treasure trove of art pieces. Some hung precariously from nails hammered into the dividing walls, but most rested overlapping each other on the compact soil floor. Every inch of space was adorned with dust-covered paintings, textiles, masks, sculptures, and religious artefacts. I was standing in the midst of the priceless outputs of Nigeria's most accomplished creatives.

The impact of Chief Oyenike Monica Okundaye, the owner and curator of several such centres and the powerhouse behind the revival of Adire textile making and dyeing, lies beneath the fame of prominent national male artists. From humble beginnings, Mama Nike inherited her weaving and Adire batik-making skills from her grandmother. Cherished for centuries, these sacred processes were lovingly woven into the close circles of family life. They became the source of female empowerment and the resource that built Mama Nike's purpose and passion in life.

A shy boy I met on the street showed me the entrance to the hidden workshop. Through a gap in a broken fence behind a twisted walnut tree, I followed a barely visible path around the back of a dilapidated building. What opened before me was Mama Nike's dream in action.

Two women were each holding an end of a long flowing piece of cloth, intricately covered in a tripled coloured design of circles and dissecting lines, allowing the wind to billow within it like a sail. They allowed it to settle next to the other pieces on the grass in the sun. The ground was covered with what looked like a mass of drying laundry of standard sheet lengths in a profusion of colours. These sheets matched the lengths of the cloths laid over the width of the tables set out in rows under the wooden shelters. Bent over each cloth was its designer, absorbed in their craft and performance of their skill. They drew freehand with wax, carefully squeezing it from the nozzle of a conical cloth bag held tightly between thumb and fingers. The collective concentration created an air of serene intensity interrupted only with occasional friendly banter and supervisory feedback. The smell of burning wax was pungent in the air.

In this production workshop concealed from the public eye, young people were being trained to design exquisite fabrics in the traditional Adire way using wax as a resister when applying the dyes. The designs were the traditional heirlooms of the Nigerian artists and were being shared with the new generation of students who chose this pathway as their vocation. Some students were on apprentice scholarships to lift them out of poverty with a guaranteed skill and work outlet, others on industrial placements from their university courses around Nigeria, and occasionally internees joined from colleges around the world. All were supervised by experienced teachers who shared their skills and oversaw the smooth running of this empowering cooperative. Everyone was involved in some aspect of the work. Some stood at saltwater-filled baths, poking long sticks onto submerged cloths covered in dried wax and richly coloured dye. Others ladled out the hot wax which had congealed on the steaming surface of vats overflowing with coloured fabric. Over by the gnarled indigo trees, the old clay dye vats lay cracked and redundant, replaced with large metal containers steaming over open wood fires. It was here that Saheed carefully stirred a bubbling cauldron of deep purple liquid.

This batch of cloth was commissioned by a German company specialising in authentic global textiles. He marvelled at how the worth of these handmade masterpieces had changed over the years. Once cloths worn in the homes and fields of the country's villagers, now fashioned into elegant costumes exhibited on catwalks around the world.

Mesmerised for a moment, I stood beside Patricia and watched her carefully lift a piece of dripping cloth from a dye pot. "And it all starts as a piece of white cloth." Her words echoed my own admiration for the revival of this art form and Mama Nike's determination to empower the new generation.

15 – CAMEROON

HONOURING THE DEAD IN BAMILÉKÉ LAND

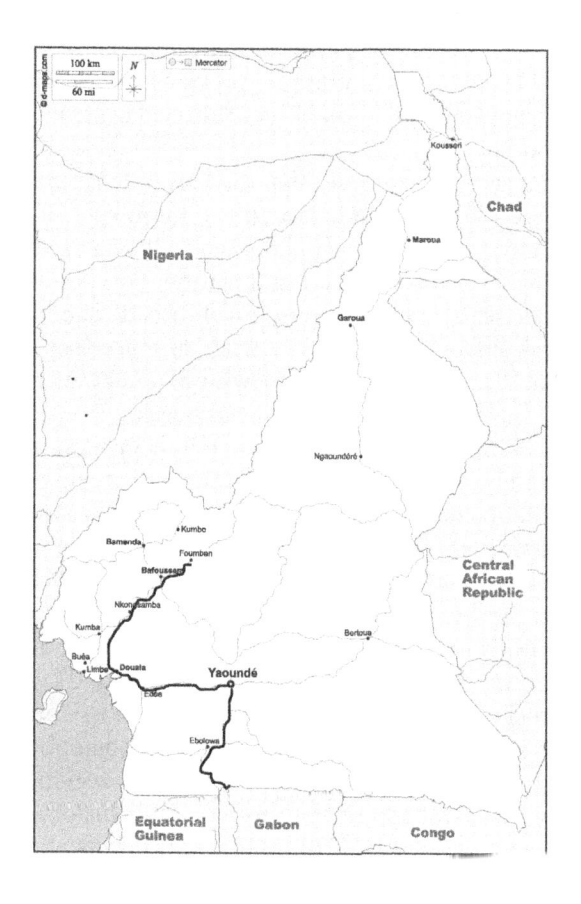

Betina led me along a path of padded earth that crossed the fields around the edge of the village. The soil was a rich rusty red colour contrasting starkly with the vibrant green of the crops. She pointed out the rows of maize and the banana plants and guava trees before we rounded the corner of a white plastered building. She called a greeting and an older woman emerged from one of the buildings clutching a bundle of firewood. Her deeply lined face lit up with joy, and she bent stiffly to place the wood on the ground before giving Betina an emotional hug. They spoke quietly in a lyrical dialect whilst Betina unloaded gifts of food from her basket. I learnt they had last seen each other the previous year when Betina had brought her husband's body to the village from Douala for his burial.

Betina was pleased to see that the flowers surrounding the grave were still being tended to. "It's all I wanted for him," she said quietly. "Lots of beautiful, coloured flowers that bloom each year – something simple and natural. We couldn't afford anything else." A solid earth mound at the side of one of their fields was surrounded by a low wooden fence that kept the goats out. This mound, covered with a canopy of reds and oranges, marked where the coffin was buried.

Betina's husband was born and raised in Bamiléké, and Betina and I were there to visit her family and attend a funeral. He and Betina had met in Germany when he was studying on a scholarship, and he told her of his wishes to return to Cameroon after his studies. In becoming his wife, she had chosen to step into another culture to raise their children. Now a widow, she remained in Douala, but wanted occasionally to make the trip up country to pay her respects at her husband's grave.

Bamiléké land is a peaceful agricultural grassland area in the west of the country, rolling close to the Anglophone area of this majority Francophone country. The region experienced much revolt and unrest throughout its history and has proudly retained many of the traditional beliefs and rituals that are deeply embedded in its customs and chiefdoms. As a long-time member of one of the Baham women's associations, Betina had been invited to a funeral celebration at a neighbouring village. She asked me to accompany her and in so doing, I would get an insight into this important event.

The banner flying above the entry to the village presented a large picture of the deceased, Souop Kamgaing David, dressed formally in a tuxedo alongside a wooden black panther with piercing green eyes. The animal totem indicated that the celebration was for a strong, brave and protective member of the village. Betina had dressed appropriately in the recognisable fabric of her association, with ceremonial beads around her neck and a hair cover that matched her floating dress. There was a unique grace in the way she carried her interculturality, making her easily recognisable to all.

We were ushered into the house of the deceased, its extensions and renovations completed with this celebration in mind. His widow showed us to the room where breakfast was laid out, and we collected eggs, bread and cake to carry out to the plastic chairs arranged under a white tent. Here sat members of Betina's women's group, identified by their shared attire, who were clearly delighted that she had travelled from the city to join them. Conversing in French, the women updated each other with news and discussed the expected programme of the day. The group then moved on. I followed as we walked past the rehearsing musicians and dancers to pay respects to the deceased's grave erected close to the house. The tomb-like construction, lined with black and white tiles, was clearly a mark of status and respect. I now understood Betina's comment made by her husband's grave.

The cook invited us to take helpings of chicken stew, foo-foo, spicy vegetable soup, spinach, and tubes of pounded maize dough wrapped in palm leaves. Handling this food with my hands and savouring the flavours was a joyful and communal occasion. Around us people gathered to join friends and community members, all dressed in their traditional and ceremonial clothes to indicate their village association, relationship to the family or role in the ceremony. There were subtle and accepted etiquettes in abundance.

It was the slow intensifying rhythmic calling of the drums accompanied by the counter motifs of the raffia rattles that drew us towards the area designated for dancing. The simply dressed musicians were already increasing the tempo and volume of their sound, dancing with arms outstretched in the centre. Around them the single file, slow-paced dance of the immediate family members had started. The leaders balanced huge bowl-shaped feather-edged hats on their heads and swayed to the rhythmic words of endearment chanted in a prayerlike mediation. Lines of women wearing identical fabrics from associations across the region simultaneously joined in, rotating around the beating core of the gathering. Some had added pictures of the deceased to the beads hanging around their heads. One line of women balanced heavy baskets filled with yams on their heads and wove their way after the others forming yet another concentric circle of bodies chanting and swaying. There were groups of men dressed in flowing gowns edged in gold thread. They wore headdresses edged with cowrie shells and waved severed horse tails to ward off evil spirits. Most of the male elders wore traditional blue and white cotton and proudly carried ceremonial swords or scabbards. I watched from the sidelines as more and more men and women joined the dancing lines of celebrators. A pageant of colours and outfit designs merged in this village scene seeped in reverence, tradition and community.

It would have been easy to miss the arrival of the secret society members. They moved silently into the peripheral space of the throngs as the drumming reached its crescendo. They slowly paced their way through the crowds before disappearing along a track at the other side of the gathering. The shaggy cloaks and long dreadlocked masks covered every inch of their bodies, hiding their identities. They represented the austere nobility of the deceased, his membership to their society, and their part in ensuring his smooth transition to become a respected ancestor within the afterlife.

Very gradually the atmosphere began to relax and soften as the drumming slowed and the chants subsided. The lines of humanity started to disperse, and people began to gather towards friends and companions. A wooden xylophone projected a melodic sound and the singing started to float over the crowds. I witnessed the natural move from intensity to normality, a sign that the ceremony was complete, and that life could continue. The necessary marking of this member's life had been carried out in abundance.

Betina and I returned to the tranquillity of her village and walked back through the fields towards her mother-in-law's house. She wanted to sit beside her husband's grave once more before we headed back to the city. "He never complained, you know, even when he was wracked with pain and unable to breathe. I like to think of him as a dove, a peace bringer and an envoy of good news."

Her gaze drifted across the fields and over towards the forest in the distance. Without turning, she began to reminisce. She spoke of the times when she and her husband would walk alone to the far edge of the forest and climb up onto the top of a huge rock. There they would sit, looking out across the valley. She remembered how they would trace the smoke trails from the village cooking fires and watch the swooping flights of the bats as the expanding sunset painted the sky. As we prepared to leave, Betina turned to me revealing damp eyes. "I love this country so much. Everything about it is integrated within me. I could never leave it now."

I wrapped my arm around her shoulders, and we headed slowly back to the village. After saying farewell to her family members, we began the long journey back to Douala.

16 – GABON

HOPES FOR LAMBARÉNÉ'S FUTURE

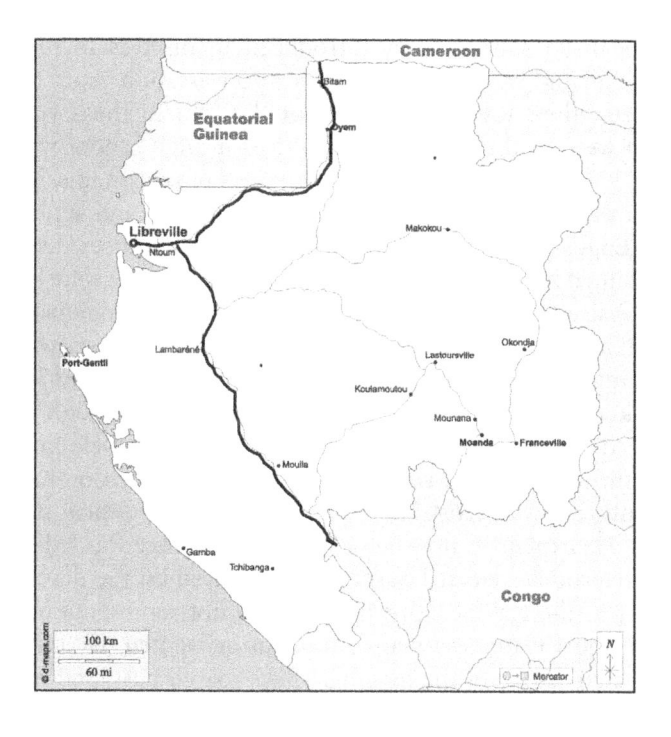

The day opened and closed with the sound of the logging trucks thundering through the town and over the bridges of the Ogooue River. Convoys consisting of eight trucks, each pulling loaded trailers filled with twelve mature tree trunks, were led by white pickups with flashing lights. The trucks followed each other closely to maximise the use of the permissible travelling windows enforced in the town. Some days

75

we would watch up to ten conveys pass through as the sun rose, followed by the same number in the evening as the sun set. Intimidated by the size and noise, people would clear the pavements and avoid the bridges to let the trucks have the right of way. A natural pattern of dominance had worked its way into the heart of the town's behaviour.

I met Ekomi and his three friends as they were walking home from school. They introduced themselves to me in German and we continued to have a conversation about their studies, their town and hopes for the future. These young men were in the final grade of the local high school where they were starting to prepare for the end of year exams. They took their studies seriously, learning in French and studying the English language as one of their chosen courses. Ekomi explained how Lambaréné, the town in which they were born and raised, had changed from being a traditional fishing town to being increasingly dependent on the Chinese-owned logging companies for employment. The boys worried what work and prospects the town could offer them, though they shared a responsibility to be part of its future development. Ekomi was the most vocal about the current situation in the country; he was frustrated by a perpetuating political situation. He explained how he believed the country was led by a predetermined elected party, which focused on the development of the capital Libreville and was not representative of what most Gabonese people thought or wanted. He turned to watch as one of the logging trucks roared past, and in an almost inaudible voice said, "There goes another load of our trees, on their way to feed the markets of China and India. Where is the investment in our country?"

On their daily walk home from school, the boys would alternate talking in English and German. Today was a German-speaking day and their science homework was the conversational topic. Ekomi explained that they teach themselves to speak German because their dream is to one day study there rather than at a university in Libreville or in France. "We meet German speaking visitors in our town. We can practice with native speakers and learn about their country. We believe we would do well there in our studies and get some work."

These German speaking visitors are predominately connected with the internship programmes and the annual conference organised at the Centre de Recherches Médicales de Lambaréné, based in the town's Albert Schweitzer Hospital. The Centre leads the research into schistosomiasis, an acute and chronic parasitic disease, which is an increasing problem for children, fishermen and young people in the Lambaréné area. The Centre has close links with the University of Tuebingen in Germany and Leiden University in the Netherlands, and hosts medical professionals and students conducting research into tuberculosis and other bacterial diseases. It is these visitors and their interactions with the young people in the town that fuel aspirations abroad and a focus on learning the German language.

When I met Ekomi and his friends again, they wanted to talk more about their hopes for the future. "We want to be active members of our community, making Lambaréné a place where tourists will want to visit. We hope to study at the university in Germany to come back to work at the hospital. Maybe we can also learn how to stop the logging. We know this is stripping our forests of wood forever and we must learn how to manage this. We think the tourists will come back soon but they need to be able to see our natural environment, the forests and the animals." The students had been open about the many issues for which they were trying to reconcile and seek solutions. There was so much potential amongst these young people, which I hoped could be harnessed in the development of the area and Gabon as a whole

17 – GABON

THE UNSUNG HERO

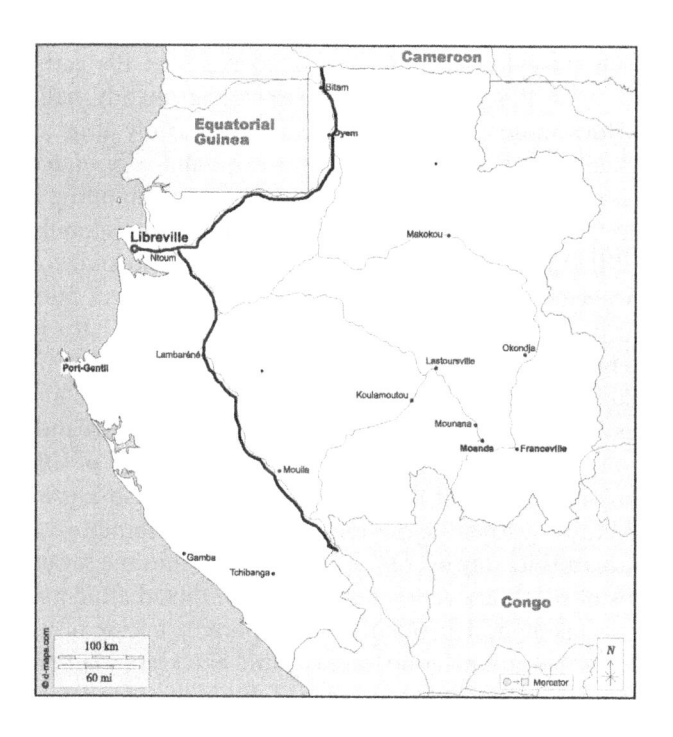

"We have three more passengers to collect," announced Youssuf in heavily accented French. He pulled his well-worn pickup truck onto a rough, potholed track and navigated the creaking vehicle towards a tin-roofed single-storey building to the right. Waiting in the shade was a bright-eyed smiling young man in a wheelchair sitting under the protruding roof of the building. His face lit up on seeing Youssuf, who stepped down from the truck and walked up to a woman standing close by. Her dark weathered face and faded patterned dress spoke of years of labour in the sun. He spoke softly as she leaned into his shoulder, gently caressing the kicking feet of the baby wrapped in a cloth on her back. The scene was one of comradeship, respect and dependency.

Youssuf helped the young man manoeuvre his chair towards the back door of the pickup and waited as he heaved himself into the seat. The young man rested his catheter, which was attached to a transparent bag already half-full of yellow liquid, on his knee. He smiled warmly at us as we checked he was comfortable. The woman and baby squeezed in beside him. The man sitting beside me was shouting loud advice to Youssuf whilst continually wiping away globules of sweat that formed below the rim of his cap. Youssouf folded the wheelchair with force and attached it to the back bumper of the pickup with a length of rope. We set off to join the main road heading east.

Youssuf's taxi service served the remote forest communities located along the untarred track between Ndendé in Gabon and Ngogo on the border with the Republic of Congo. It was the first leg of my journey to Dolisie (also known as Loubomo), a town at the end of this 276-kilometre artery that threads its way over forest clad massifs into the savannah plains of the Niari Valley. Settlements of mixed ethic groups live alongside it, dependent on the sporadic trickle of traffic for trade, communication, security and emergency support. I was soon to learn the importance of this lifeline for its people and their suspicious dread of the looming inevitability of any developmental project planned to widen and tarmac most of its length.

As we approached the end of Ndendé's main street, a man jumped out of a shelter by the roadside shouting unintelligible words at Youssuf. Our driver calmly negotiated some deal with him, leading to an exchange of money and the immediate emergence of nine teenage football players from behind a fence. Still clothed in their kit and chattering excitedly about their game of the previous evening, the young players jumped into the back of the truck. The vehicle was now full and together we were a motley crew of fifteen, all heading to the border.

I soon began to marvel at Youssuf's driving skills and tenacity. He sped along the dry, smooth sections of the track and slowed to calculate the best pathways through the gravel, ruts and the flooded streams. All obstacles were managed with the mastery and steadiness of a professional. I was in awe! Along the way, he stopped to wish people well and drop off the provisions of rice, oil and building parts lodged under the feet of the football team in the back. At one home, we stopped to greet a man who hugged Youssuf as one would a long-lost friend. Alongside some limes and potatoes arranged on a small wooden table by the roadside, he had hung a yellow and green striped iguana on a stick. This piece of choice bushmeat soon found its place in the rear of the truck; a welcomed purchase for a family back in Ndendé.

Just before the border, we stopped beside two detached single-storey tin-roofed homesteads set back from the road in the shade of the dense forest. A cluster of children ran from where they were chopping firewood and preparing food in a huge black pot to gather beside the truck. They peered expectantly through the rear window to catch a glimpse of their brother, mother and baby sibling. The wheelchair was untied and brought to the door where the still smiling passenger carefully swung himself from the vehicle into the chair. It was clear that this scenario was new. A male family member struggled to push the rickety wheelchair up and over the gravelly ground from the road to the house. Here the children flocked around their brother and welcomed him home from the clinic in Ndendé. I couldn't help but wonder what the future held for him and what support the family would have.

The life of this roadside community continued to unfold as we drove on. At a spot along the road where there were no homesteads or people in sight, my seat companion suddenly disconnected his phone charger from the dashboard and jumped out. He sped off into the forest undergrowth heading for his brother's home, which was somewhere in the middle of it all. He had told me they had some money matters to deal with, and his family members were in dispute. He hoped they would find a solution. "I'll see you in three days' time for a lift back," were his parting words to Youssuf, spoken in Fang, one of their shared languages.

At Doussala the pickup truck stopped, and preparations were made for the last stretch to the border. This involved decanting the football team who were asked to walk the last kilometre. This would apparently enable the truck to pass over the border without issues with the police. The players could join us again once past the checkpoints. Four new passengers joined us after relieving themselves beside the roadside and we set off in a cloud of dust.

Ngongo, the border crossing, consisted of a cluster of government administration rooms, ramshackle huts posing as shops selling provisions, and a couple of bars. Loud music played from one and women ran out with plastic bottles filled with palm wine and Fanta to drum up business. Youssuf was clearly a celebrity here and was guided off by an animated restaurateur to share a beer and some food. His passengers meanwhile were directed to the passport office to get the necessary stamp for admission into the Republic of the Congo. It was here that I met the chief of police, who reconfirmed the importance of Youssuf's taxi service.

"Youssuf is a gentleman – a true Teke. Reliable, knowledgeable about our people and always helpful. I trust him, he brings our official documents in his truck. Here, there is no divide between the people living on the Gabon and Congo sides – we are one community, helping each other."

Once through the formalities and refreshed with freshly made food, we were rounded up to continue our journey. Due to the condition of the roads, Youssuf was going to take us as far as the next village where shared taxis in old Renault cars would be available for the rest of the journey. He knew his vehicle was the only one that could get through the next section of the track, so the community had just adjusted the changeover location. Along this section, we said goodbye to members of the football team as we neared their homes. They were going to be sharing the triumphs of yesterday's win against the youth team of Ndendé with their friends. These young players, aided by the respective police officers, refused let a border crossing interfere with their regular fixtures with the nearest football team.

As for myself and the other passengers, our parting gift from Youssuf was the smooth transfer into the care of Carlos, our driver for the next leg of the journey from Nyanga to Dolisie. Another adventure and story to tell.

18 - THE REPUBLIC OF THE CONGO

DO YOU CRY?

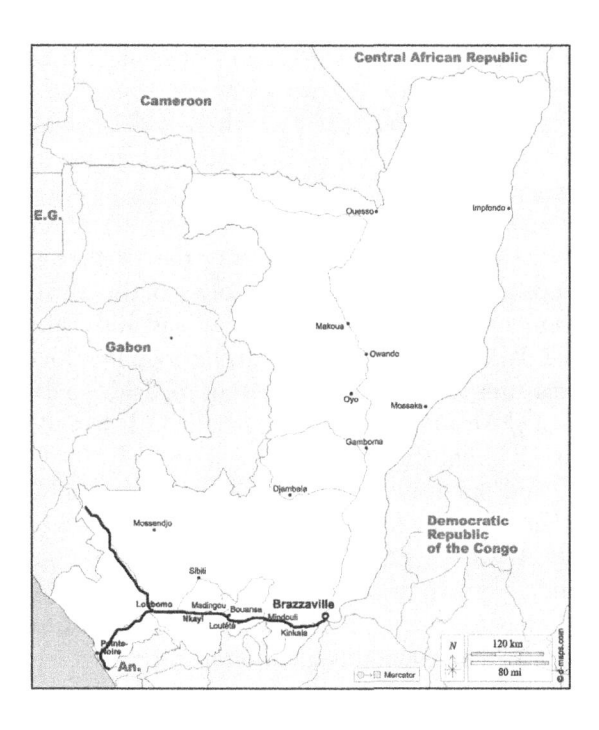

We had been waiting at the gare de routière in Dolisie for the sixth passenger to show up before we could all get back on the road. After Patrick squeezed in beside me on the back seat, the driver tightened the rope securing the hatchback door over the bulging boot at the back. He then drove the car over the potholed forecourt and pulled out into the main street of Dolisie, heading for Pointe-Noire on the coast.

At first Patrick and I exchanged our introductions in French. He was returning home to Pointe-Noire after doing business in Dolisie. He managed a logistics company that distributed food, construction materials and clothing. Goods were imported from the Democratic Republic of the Congo and Gabon at the port based at Pointe-Noire and distributed to companies based in Brazzaville and other towns inland. He explained about the improvements to the road we were travelling along. "This hundred and fifty-eight kilometres of road was a dirt track until two years ago. It used to take an entire day to get between the two towns, and we would often get stuck in mud or move trees that had fallen across the road. It was in very poor condition."

The road that now wound up through thick rainforest towards the summit of the range skirting the coastline was fully tarmacked and well maintained. "Another of the construction improvements built by the Chinese," I was told. It began to rain, and darkness descended quickly through the clouds.

It was after we stopped by a row of roadside stalls to buy bottles of Coke and Fanta that Patrick and I began to chat in English. His English language skills were far better than my French, and our conversation flowed more naturally. As we settled back into our confined space in the car, he asked unexpectedly whether I ever cried. The question was asked with no agenda or provocation, just a natural part of our exchange. I noted how it seemed quite organic in this context, but how odd if I would be asked this question in Europe.

"I do cry – when I'm sad, when I miss my family and if I'm in pain. Sometimes I cry with joy when I see something magical, beautiful or loving. What about you, do you cry?"

It is always interesting to know where such a question would come from and why it would be asked. I sat back and waited to hear more. Patrick slowly began to share information about his life that was precious and humbling.

"I cried when my wife gave birth to our twins last week. They are healthy and beautiful – we are blessed by God with five children." He reached for his phone and showed me a video of the newborn twins in a cradle next to his wife in the hospital. The video captured an intimate moment in his life, and he shared it with openness and joy. "My wife is still in hospital. I will visit her tomorrow as it will be too late in the day when we arrive."

The exchange brought a closeness and easy companionship to this carload of strangers travelling through the night. I noticed how Patrick and the other passengers encouraged and supported the driver as he carefully navigated the twists in the road whilst we descended towards the coast. Thunder and lightning pierced the darkness as the rain intensified. Water was forming a flowing veneer over the tarmac. We became silent as the steam from the road obscured our visibility and our driver slowed to a crawl to avoid skids and unlit obstacles. Our collective assurance for a safe journey urged him on.

As we drove onto a more level road heading towards the coast our driver visibly relaxed, the music returned, and conversation resumed. The passengers made sure I saw the flames of the new Pointe-Noire oil refineries, which we caught glimpses of as the forest thinned. The scattered lights of the approaching town intensified, and the road became rutted with muddy tracks. The passengers welcomed me to their hometown, the next step on my journey.

The driver finally pulled up at the Marché de Tie-Tie in the old part of town. The ground was wet and muddy, and the air was damp. Patrick bid us farewell and disappeared into the crowds. The other passengers hauled their luggage from the boot and onto the back of motorbike taxis. There were no lights or visible waiting areas just a muddle of fast-moving bodies eager to get out of the soaking rain.

Eventually I managed to find a taxi and we headed through town towards the beach area to my hotel. The taxi weaved through the congested streets and bounced over the railway tracks by the dilapidated railway station. As I walked towards the reception, I felt the sterility of this bland business hotel. It seemed so far removed from the warm bubble of humanity I had just experienced in our shared taxi. It reminded me of how fleeting such memorable moments can be and how important it is to treasure them.

19 – ANGOLA

THE POWER OF NATURE

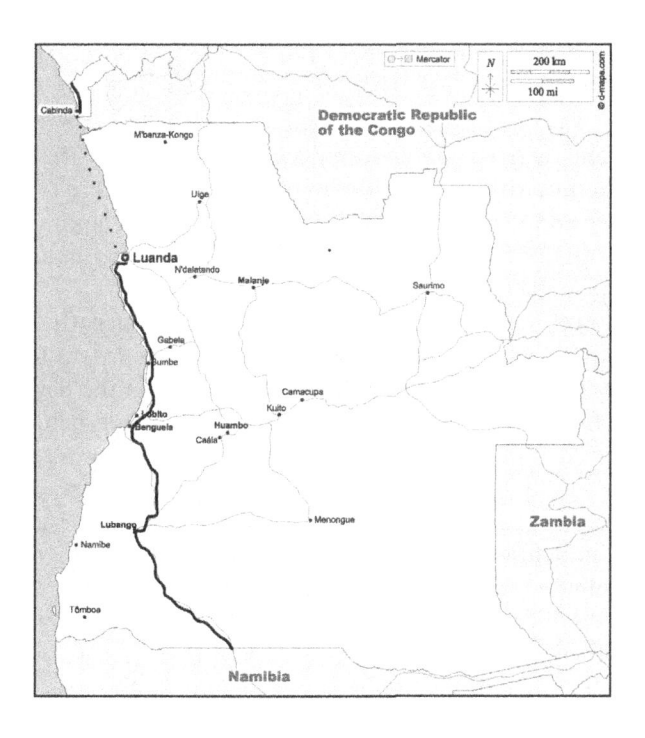

Christo Rei de Lubango stands on a hillside overlooking the city of the same name in Angola. His gaze drops towards the urban area in the valley and his wide-open arms try to embrace the spread of its development. The statue's height and gleaming marble brightness sends an impressive sense of authority mixed with benevolence down on the humanity living beneath. It is a grand reminder that a percentage of this city's population descended from the Madeira Portuguese settlers who migrated to Lubango back in the late 1800s, bringing their religion and cultural practices with them. The Christ the King statue was inspired by Christ the Redeemer in Rio de Janeiro, and the construction was the Catholic way of acknowledging the new independent era in 1975, an enduring backdrop to the city.

Lubango provided a relaxed and culturally diverse stopover enroute to the Nambian border. Originally established as a settlement named after an ancient Soba chief, the town's name was changed to Sá da Bandeira when the Portuguese migrants arrived. Their influence was evident in the integrated mix within its people, architecture and culture today. I conversed in Portuguese, visited the old colonial buildings in the centre of town and sampled a fusion of food with distinct European flavours.

However, it was the scenery beyond Lubango that surprised me. Its dramatic, geographic magnificence was totally unexpected. I sat on the side of a gorge within the Serra da Leba mountain range, looking out across the plains below the escarpment that skirts the coast. The craggy cliffs were home to numerous native birds and small animals and an abundance of butterflies. Watching my enjoyment of the nature laid out before me was a young boy who stepped towards me swinging a caged blue breasted waxbill, hoping for a quick sale. Who was I to tell him I would prefer the bird to fly free?

Flowing through a gap in the rocks is the ten kilometre stretch of road linking Lubango to Namibe on the coast. This dramatic piece of engineering switches round more than sixty hairpin bends to drop from the plano alto at 1,845 metres to the plains below at sea level. Legend says that Maria Alice Leba designed and oversaw its build to completion, passing away the same day it opened. She rests in peace knowing that the decade it took to construct the road was worthwhile. Vehicles wind carefully up and down its well-maintained length, manoeuvring themselves around the unguarded bends.

Another spectacular natural form within the rim of the escarpment was the Tundavala Gap, the Fenda da Tundavala. A deep abyss had formed between the rocks, framing a breathtaking view towards the coast. A newly constructed viewing point invited visitors to get close to the edge and gaze down into the depths of the vertigo-inducing gorge. The sound of bells announced the arrival of a herd of cows that had wandered close to the escarpment edge seeking fresh grass. The herder walked behind them gently guiding them onwards. The whole area breathed antiquity, an endless sense of time and nature's power.

20 – NAMIBIA

ON DIAMONDS WE BUILD

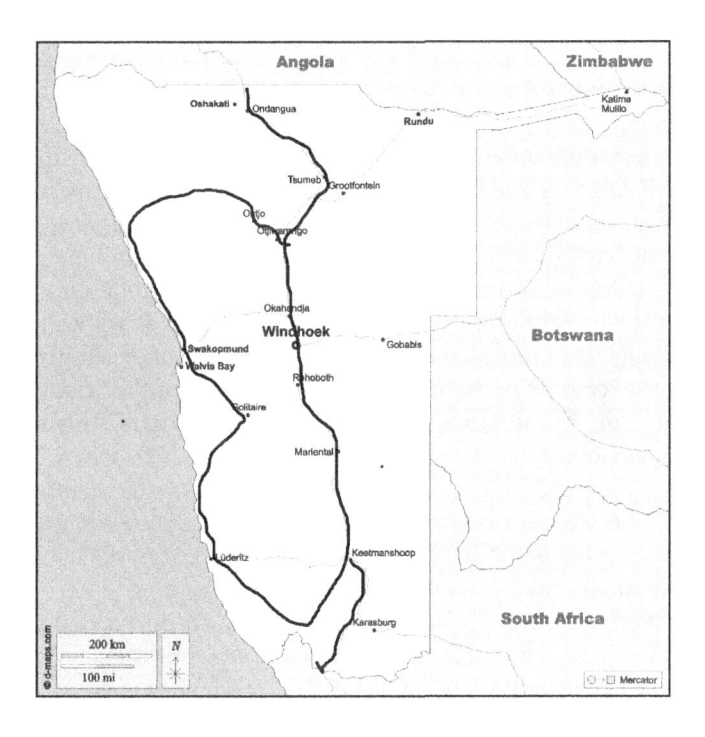

The director of the 1929 cult horror film, *Dust Devil*, clearly saw the atmospheric potential of this setting in the desert. He used it as the backdrop for the contentious film's last moments, to accentuate sentiments of courage and tragedy laced with fear. As I walked through the ghost town of Kolmanskop, these emotions seemed to spill out from its surreal remains now left struggling to breathe under the sea of ever-rising sand. There was a sense of dark inevitability in the silent nostalgia cloaking the abandoned buildings and its history.

The tour guide was laughing with a group of sweating South African motorcyclists, newly arrived from their adventurous journey north from Cape Town. Their Afrikaans reverberated around one of the buildings, and I picked out words referring to fishing and shovelling their machines out of sand dunes. The rest of us stood waiting for explanations.

We were in an area with buildings similar to the village community centres of 1930s England, with heavily curtained stages, balcony mezzanines, free-standing piped organs, and leather topped gym equipment. "The German mine owners, their families and European workers would congregate here for meals, celebrations, church services and shows. That room at the back was a smoking space for men, and behind me was the champagne bar for the ladies." Our tour guide continued to reveal descriptions of the town's prime as we walked through the renovated rooms and buildings, as if on a film set. In the ice making room, we were introduced to the scientific ingenuity of the 1900s water freezing technologies. This was followed by a visit to the sausage making kitchens where the tarnished equipment and monstrous ovens lay dormant. In the shopkeeper's house, our guide painted pictures of grandeur, opulence and abundance with inferences of favours provided for the owner's scrupulous bookkeeping.

Perhaps it was the description of the town's open sided taxi service pulled along the short shopping street by donkeys that completed the unnatural scene. The resident women of the time would be chauffeured home from their shopping expeditions along with their rations of ice, lemonade and braadworst. In the evenings, we were told, the bar in the main street would serve chilled bottled beers and brandies, whilst the adjacent bowling alley thudded with the bounce of wooden balls. Up on the hillside a walled open aired pool of desalinated water would beckon restless children.

The guide continued to add historical information: Kolmanskop was hastily erected on the spontaneous wealth that flowed into the area when diamonds were discovered in 1908. The Sperrgebiet Diamond Mine was established, and the excavation and trading were monopolised and controlled by the De Beers Consolidated Diamond Mines Company. As its Namibian headquarters, Kolmanskop boasted an extraction and preparation mining plant, a large hospital with an x-ray machine, and a school delivering lessons in German. It was a home from home built on diamonds.

However, the tour felt strangely incomplete. Looking down into the valley below Kolmanskop, one could not help but notice the remains of the town, currently off limits, on heavily policed and fenced land. Within sight were the rows of low buildings that had provided living accommodation, an eating hall, a medical clinic, and a shop for hundreds of male Nambian and migrant workers who came here on employment contracts of two years. "Each new employee was quarantined on arrival, not allowed home leave within each contract, and given regular laxatives to stop diamonds being swallowed internally," explained our guide. Perhaps we were skirting around the real source of the sentiments of courage and tragedy blowing in these desert winds.

For almost 50 years, Kolmanskop thrived as a mine and a community. Lives were lived, memories created, and money earned, and then the focus shifted south. More lucrative diamond reserves enticed its occupants towards Oranjemund, and the community moved on. Now the abandoned town has become a tourist attraction and a fashionable location for film makers. Kolmanskop is owned by NAMDEB, a Namibian government and De Beers Company venture, which continues to build enterprises on its diamonds. Hopefully these guided tours will soon tell a fuller story of the inhabitants of Kolmanskop.

21 – SOUTH AFRICA

MEMORIES IN A COOKBOOK

The District 6 Museum proudly occupied a Former Mission Methodist church, providing a space for former residents to engage in creative projects. Part of the converted property, located on Buitenkant Street in Cape Town, incorporated a corridor that ran the length of the chapel's prayer hall and shared the wall that had once supported the organ. In the past, the corridor had led to the vestibules used by the methodist preachers and their assistants, however it now provided wall space for a collection of memorabilia that was last exhibited to the public in February 2016.

Hand embroidered panels hung on the walls on either side of the corridor. Their delicate stitching depicted food dishes, ingredients and decorative features, with framed handwritten inlays outlining the details of recipes, recommended food stores and culinary tips. I was struck by the alluring simplicity of each panel, almost childlike in their presentation. A closer read however revealed complex recipes embedded in life stories. There was a sugar bean curry recipe from Omartjies Café, said to be the tastiest in all of District 6. Next was a recipe for melktert, a delicious pastry crust with a custard filling, offered as a grandmother's speciality and enjoyed at afternoon tea parties. Further down the wall were the details of how to cook roast chicken, with an added note that in the 1940s and 50s chicken was a luxury so this would have been for Sunday lunch only. This was clearly more than a collection of recipes. Each one reflected a bygone age and carried the nostalgia of family life, culture, and the socioeconomic backgrounds of a mixed community.

I followed the corridor and found the handwritten biographies of the creators; each giving a name, family details, and some contextual black and white photographs to provide a window into their lives. These stories, written in black ink, were displayed on unmounted paper and seemed to me to project a vulnerable sense of fragility. Each one spoke of simple ingredients, locally based markets, and ways to feed a large family.

The recipe panels and penned biographies formed the exhibition 'Huis Kombuis – the food of District 6', a design project where storytelling, performance, and traditional craftwork involving embroidery, sewing and applique work were used to document the culinary life of a past era. It was launched 50 years after the District 6 area of central Cape Town was declared a white group area and the original families were rehoused outside of the city.

This 'Huis Kombuis' project had enabled women to come together to pool their experiences and re-appropriate them into a beautiful record of their homebased crafts, traditions and cultures. As the curator summarised, "This project brought women together to talk and share their memories and skills; it was a healing process and a validation of the vibrant community they once contributed to."

The museum's activities told a powerful story of what can happen when imposed policies change people's lives forever. The creative projects and the voluntary ex-resident guides recount evidence of the vibrancy of the community that once lived in District 6, before it was slowly deconstructed due to the rehousing policies of the 1960s and 70s. Their overall message was a call for the dignity, identity and the co-existence of different races and backgrounds to be respected now and into the future.

As asserted by one of the ex-resident guides, "Our community in District 6 was destroyed, but we have survived, and we have excelled despite apartheid. Our families are the future of South Africa."

EPILOGUE

I arrived at my final destination, Cape Town, courtesy of the intercity bus from Windhoek, Namibia. A feeling of personal achievement mixed with a slight disbelief that I had made it to the end point buoyed me on through the first days in the city. The thrill of another new place to explore also distracted me from the reality of reaching the end of this phase in my life's journey, and the need to face what was next.

The last ten months were an incredible time of learning, an opportunity to see life from a different viewpoint. I acquired knowledge and insights through numerous experiences and conversations. These authentic, trusting, and candid encounters often challenged my biases, assumptions and inherited mental models. They helped me build an awareness and knowledge base that I was committed to expand.

My many conversations with historians, researchers, and fellow educators heighten the need to redress the balance of knowledge and the perceptions taught in schools on the African continent as well as beyond. These professionals passionately advocate for a rethink of curriculum content and a change of pedagogy. They share a belief that learners need more exposure to a balance of researched facts and open debate. We are bound by a common responsibility to influence curriculum design globally.

Interconnecting themes emerged as I moved across borders that deserved further exploration. I was able to connect with entrepreneurs of all ages, backgrounds, and political affiliations. Most were actively developing small scale locally based enterprises. These focused on agricultural diversity, artisan empowerment, environmental sustainability, financial mobility, technological advancement, and community welfare. I was fascinated by the capacity for scalable development that was building within the emerging infrastructures of their countries. The web of trade in knowledge, skill, finance, and output was intriguing.

My curiosity was well and truly ignited. Travelling tends to do that, acting as a mirror and reflecting new learning as well as providing insights into what is always considered to be familiar. I learnt to reframe my previous life experiences and rethink what I thought I knew.

These months of travelling brought me a liberating sense of freedom. I learnt to set intentions, plan more loosely and embrace flexibility. New opportunities evolved daily, and I stepped into these more readily. I prioritised safety, connection and harmony, and moved away from expecting adhered schedules and immediate responses. Frequently my assumptions were different to the resulting outcome. I learnt to accept these and relax into the flow of the journey, to trust the process. I vowed to integrate these qualities into the next phase of my life, wherever I was based.

Travelling alone brought spontaneous opportunities. I understood the importance of trusting my intuition more, knowing that I knew what was right for myself and how to move forwards. I connected with diverse groups of people and in doing so was rewarded with heartwarming exchanges of personal stories, family legacies and life lessons. People helped me to see my experiences from a wide range of perspectives and to overcome inhibitions of my language skills, background and status.

I began to appreciate that my whole experience in western Africa would influence the way I would live the next stage of my life. I knew I would endeavour to take a more simplistic view, to strip away the immaterial, and to keep the focus on the fundamentals. I knew that my memoirs of the past months would be good reminders to keep stepping beyond the familiar, keep connecting with different people, and to remain open to questioning my own assumptions and perspectives about life. In reaching South Africa, I had fulfilled a dream. It also became the place where the seeds for the next idea were sown. I had rediscovered my curiosity for exploring the world and was ready to embrace its next adventure.

THANK YOU EVERYONE

Thank you to all the people I met on the road. Although I was a stranger you trusted me with your time, openness and stories. In those moments of connection, you proved that we can all learn from each other with or without a common language and background. There is so much love, joy and appreciation within our humanity.

Thank you to my family and friends who continually asked me to write about my travels. Thank you for relentlessly nudging me to start this process and believing that my adventures are worth sharing.

Thank you to Kate, for generously sharing your own journey as a writer. You helped me to see this possibility in myself, creating the space and guidance for it to emerge.

Thank you to June, for telling your own journey as a traveller and writer. I feel seen by you. You have taught me the value of speaking and writing about my experiences.

Thank you to Max, for responding to my call for help with editing and for bringing accuracy and style to my writing approach.

Lastly, thank you to Shân and Karen, for delighting in my adventures as if they were your own. Your 'whoops for joy' and emojis always make me smile.

ABOUT THE AUTHOR

Sue Aspinall lives in the Netherlands. She has worked in England, Malaysia, Japan, and the Netherlands as a Headteacher, and now prioritises her time travelling, writing and speaking about her encounters on the road.

She spreads a message of hope for the future; referencing real-life stories that encourage us to be bold, trust in the goodness of others, and to embrace life as an ever-evolving adventure.

Made in United States
North Haven, CT
06 July 2024